HOLD ON TO
LOVE

The Relentless, Rescuing, and Restoring
Love of Our Good Father

NICHOLE MARBACH

In *Hold On to Love*, Nichole presents the heart of the Father and His great love for mankind beautifully. Her testimony, honesty, and passion to see others set free shines throughout the book. I am always encouraged to see the scriptures presented with such clarity and simplicity. I believe this book will bless and encourage many hearts and lead them into a greater understanding of the absolute freedom and security in God, who loves us all unconditionally and without reservation or hidden agendas.

Arthur Meintjes
Founder, Kingdom Life Ministry

Hold On To Love takes readers to the very heart of freedom: the love demonstrated for us when Jesus took all of our shame, condemnation, sickness, failure, abuse, addiction, self-hatred, pain, and suffering at the cross. No one is beyond the reach of God's extravagant love and the superabundance of the grace that has been poured out on us through the cross of Jesus Christ. Nichole has laid it all out, verse by verse, in this excellent treasure. I believe many will be healed as the Word goes forth in all the power of the gospel!

Tricia Gunn
Founder, Parresia and author of Unveiling Jesus

Nichole has done an amazing job inviting us into her understanding of the love of God, which rescued her from a horrible pit. This book is a walk into the Father's loving embrace. Her genuineness, humor, and transparency shine through every page of this book. I would suggest it to anyone who is interested in experiencing the Father's love in a deeper way.

Jeremiah L Johnson
Jeremiah Johnson Ministries

I have had the privilege of being friends with and ministering side by side with Nichole for several years now. I've walked through and been there with her as she's experienced and shared the powerful truths in this book, *Hold On to Love*, with people all over the world. It's such an honor to share life with her and watch people set free as she shares her testimony and her continued walk with God.

We all struggle with searching for our purpose in life sometimes. In this book, Nichole shares her story and struggles as she continues to walk out her freedom from the bondage of believing a false identity, while she holds on to her true identity as a loved and cherished daughter of God. As it is with all of us, everyday battles have tried to rip her hands off of the lifeline of knowing she is completely, unconditionally safe and loved by God. Her life's goal is to share her story to help others know the truth and find freedom as she has.

I seriously could hear her very voice in my head as I read the powerful words on the pages of this amazing book. Every word oozes the love of God and His opinion of us. You'll be transformed as you read it and realize that God did everything for us, and all we need to do is believe He loves us that much! *Hold On to Love* continues Nichole's victorious walk with Jesus, as He has never let go of her. Within its pages, she shares how He'll never let go of us either. Living loved by God is how we were created to live. We can and will experience a life of beauty and victory if we embrace who He says we are, hold on to His love, and never let go.

Christy Rose
Public Speaker and Minister of the Gospel of Jesus Christ

DEDICATION

I would like to dedicate this book to my heavenly Father, who is the most amazing and loving Father anyone could want. Discovering His relentless, rescuing, and restoring love has been the biggest healing in my life. My desire is for the world to come to know just how good You are.

I would also like to dedicate this book to the most important people in my life: my husband, Claude; my three children; and my spiritual mom, Melanie. I love you with all of my heart!

TABLE OF CONTENTS

ACKNOWLEDGMENTS

I would like to say thank you to my editor, Renée Gray-Wilburn, for doing such a phenomenal job editing this book. I am grateful for you.

"If you'll hold on to me for dear life," says GOD,
"I'll get you out of any trouble.
I'll give you the best of care
if you'll only get to know and trust me.
Call me and I'll answer, be at your side in bad times;
I'll rescue you, then throw you a party.
I'll give you a long life,
give you a long drink of salvation!"
(Psalm 91:14–16, MSG)

INTRODUCTION

I wrote *Hold On to Love* with the goal of mentoring others in the truths from God's Word that have helped me hold on to and maintain my freedom—the truth of who God says we are; who God says He is; and His relentless, rescuing, and restoring love for all of mankind.

Hold On to Love is meant to be a sequel of sorts to my prior book, *Hold On to Hope*, in which I share my true life story of finding healing and freedom in Jesus Christ. I demonstrate, through my own desperate circumstances, that no one is beyond hope and no situation is impossible for God. *Hold On to Hope* gives hope to the hopeless and sets people free who have been diagnosed with what the world calls "incurable mental illnesses." This book is now helping people to have more compassion for their loved ones who are suffering and is restoring hope that their loved ones can also walk in the same healing and wholeness that I've found in Christ.

If you have not yet read *Hold On to Hope*, I encourage you to do so to better understand the depths from which God rescued me and the healing He brought me into. This healing, provided by His amazing love, is the foundation for *Hold On to Love*.

I pray that after reading this book, you'll effortlessly fall deeper in love with our good Father and receive the indescribable love He

has for you; and, as a result, you'll be able to fully love yourself
and who He created you to be. As you receive His love, freedom
will just happen for you. I promise. I believe that receiving the
Father's love is what brings us the most healing and supernatu-
rally breaks negative mindsets we may have.

Because we live in such a negative world, it's important to continually fill ourselves with His precious Word. The Bible will
unveil Jesus to us and show us His true, loving nature. *Hold On
to Love* is just one tool to help you in your journey to freedom.

Before we get started, I'd like to share a story about my rescue
Sheltie named Beau. At the time of this writing, we've had Beau
almost six months, and he is four-and-a-half years old. He had
been passed from home to home and was previously sold off
a website notorious for selling stolen dogs. The rescue shelter
found him on this site and immediately purchased him. I was
told that the person who sold him was someone you wouldn't
want to meet in a dark alley. It was clear that the sole motive in
owning Beau was money and that he wasn't at all cared for.

We weren't surprised to learn that Beau was abused, and his
behavior confirmed it. He'd shrink back and try to nip at our
veterinarian as she gently examined him. And, when I tried pick-
ing him up to love on him, he couldn't look me in the eyes. It was
obvious that he was very uncomfortable and was anticipating
something bad happening to him. He's like a big teddy bear in
many ways, and I can't imagine anyone wanting to hurt him. It's
heart wrenching trying to show him affection, while seeing his
eyes close in fear because he thinks I'm going to hit him.

He's also afraid of the noise the gas stove makes when being lit, as well as the sound of packing tape being unrolled. It could be that one of his multiple previous owners taped his mouth closed. That's often what people do to Shelties because they're notorious barkers. Also, once when my husband was changing his clothes, he removed his belt, and Beau shrunk back in fear, terrorized. This made us so sad.

We feel it's like a ministry, but a joy, to continually love Beau and show him that he's now safe. Even though we never gave him an opportunity to think we'd abuse him, he still has a "fear mindset" that he's going to be mistreated. However, as time goes on and he trusts us more and more, his fearful reactions are subsiding. The other day, for the first time ever, I was able to pick him up and lay him on me as I sat on the couch. I held him, hugged him, and pet him. I had tried that many times before, but he was always uncomfortable and wanted to get down. However, this day, I heard him sigh, and I could tell he was comfortable, at peace, and receiving my love because he finally felt safe.

When Beau starts showing his teeth in fear, I say to him in a loving voice, "You're a nice boy," while caressing the top of his head. I'll say it over and over, and he'll eventually stop. He doesn't understand what I'm saying, but when I talk in a soothing and loving voice, he knows that he's loved and safe in that moment. He's learning more and more each day how loved and safe he truly is, which causes his outward behavior to change for the positive. Love and safety are effortlessly changing Beau.

Like Beau, people who've been abused, especially for many years, react in the same manner of fear and anxiety. There are certain mindsets that are created from abuse (I share how this happened to me in *Hold On to Hope*). These mindsets take time to change. It takes an atmosphere of consistent love by the Father and trustworthy people to break off fear and mistrust toward God and others. It's a process, which is okay. Process isn't a bad thing.

It's important to give yourself and others grace in the journey of healing and to allow the Father to love you and your loved ones through His Word, this book, and other sources. The Father's consistent love and the support of trustworthy people that He places in our life help change those negative, abusive mindsets to the truth of how He sees us.

We weren't created to live this life alone. Family and relationships were God's ideas. I'm grateful for the wonderful people the Father has placed in my life at just the right time. People who encourage me, speak truth, love me for who I am, and walk alongside me. I do the same for them. We also extend grace to each other when needed.

For years, I had a very skewed view of love based on my childhood. It took experiencing the Father's love and the love of safe people to change my perception, and I'm still growing in this. Once you realize your true heavenly worth and value, you'll stop tolerating abuse in any form, and you'll no longer chase people who don't know your value. We weren't created to be abused. We were created to be loved.

As you read this book, I pray you'll hold on to the truth and freedom that's yours in Jesus Christ. The truths that I'll be sharing have helped me since receiving the miraculous healing of bipolar disorder, depression, and self-destruction. They've helped me maintain over twelve years of freedom from mental illness and addictions. Have I fully "arrived" yet? No, I'm still growing, but I've left where I was, and I'll continue to allow the truths of God's Word to renew my mind until I leave this earth.

I talk often about our "right standing" with God in this book, which comes from faith in Jesus. It's important to understand that we're right with God, even when we fail, and to remind ourselves that we're righteous in His sight. Knowing who we are and what we have is the key to the triumphant Christian life. Knowing whose we are is life changing.

I'd like to encourage you to know that the Father is saying to you today, "I chose you without a doubt, in a heartbeat, to be My cherished and treasured child forever. I would choose you over and over again." Will you dare to believe that right now? It's the first step to receiving your freedom and healing.

Pray with me before diving into this wonderful adventure of discovering the relentless love that our good God has for you:

> *Heavenly Father, I want to know You more and more as my good Daddy in my life, who always has my best interests at heart. Thank You for helping me receive the truth that You love me, that I'm forgiven and accepted with no condemnation, that You're my rescuing Father who loves to help me, and that nothing can separate me from Your love. Father, I pray that You would help me to hold on to these truths, especially when accusing voices of condemnation try to take root in my heart. I desire to know Your relentless, rescuing, and restoring love for me. Amen!*

CHAPTER 1

THE PASSIONATE LOVE OF THE CROSS

Years ago, God led me to study what Jesus experienced on the cross. Afterward, I understood exactly why He wanted me to do this. When I was in the middle of the bipolar disorder that I thought was my cross to bear, I posed a question to the teacher at our church: "Does Jesus understand what it's like to be bipolar and to experience mental torment and abuse?"

I thought I was wise in asking this, and the teacher had no idea what to say. By doing this study, I effortlessly fell deeper in love with Jesus when I realized that He went through the pain and suffering of the cross to set me free and to reconcile me to the Father. He gets it! He understands everything that we go through. He has been there, done that, so to speak.

Since that time, I have taught this message to many groups, which have been blessed by it. As you read what Jesus went through, you shouldn't feel any condemnation or guilt; rather, reach out to experience Jesus' passionate love for you. This study changed my life, and I pray that you receive a life-changing revelation as well.

We need to begin at the cross because the cross changes everything for us. People can sometimes get annoyed when they hear of Jesus' suffering on the cross, and ask, "What about the resurrection?" I agree that we should also discuss how Jesus didn't stay on that cross once He gave up His spirit. He rose again, and we rose with Him! That's great news! But there can be no resurrection without first going to the cross.

The cross helps us see that Jesus understands everything we go through, and He has nothing but compassion and love for us. We can always turn to Him in our time of need. He understands. But, He wants to get us to the other side of freedom.

The following discussion is based on what researchers believe happened to Jesus during the final hours of His earthly life. They arrived at their conclusions from Bible passages and over fifty years of research on crucifixions during the time Jesus walked the earth. I will be using excerpts from the book, *The Crucifixion of Jesus: A Forensic Inquiry*, by Frederic T. Zugibe, M.D., Ph.D., along with scriptures, and my own study observations.

Jesus Understands Agony

Have you ever felt grief and sadness to the point of mental exhaustion? Have you ever felt pain to the point of having thoughts of dying? Jesus understands.

> **John 15:13, AMP**—"No one has greater love [nor stronger commitment] than to lay down his own life for his friends."

Although Jesus is God, He also came as a man and endured the cross as a man. Keep this thought in mind as we continue through this chapter.

Hebrews 2:15–18, TPT—

"[15]By embracing death Jesus sets free those who live their entire lives in bondage to the tormenting dread of death. [16]For it is clear that he didn't do this for the angels, but for all the sons and daughters of Abraham. [17]This is why he had to be a Man and take hold of our humanity in every way. He made us his brothers and sisters and became our merciful and faithful King-Priest before God; as the One who removed our sins to make us one with him. [18]He suffered and endured every test and temptation, so that he can help us every time we pass through the ordeals of life."

Since all of God's "children" have flesh and blood, Jesus became human to fully identify with us. He did this so He could experience death and annihilate the effects of the intimidating accuser (Satan), who holds against us the power of death.

The story of the cross begins with Jesus in the Garden of Gethsemane. *Gethsemane* literally means "oil press."[1] Just as olives have to be crushed and pressed in order to make olive oil, Jesus was crushed on this day.

Jesus took His friends (disciples) with Him to the garden, and then went to pray by Himself. He was deeply distressed—to the point that He told His disciples, "My heart is overwhelmed with anguish and crushed with grief. It feels as though I'm dying. Stay here and keep watch with me" (Mark 14:34, TPT).

His disciples fell asleep while He prayed, and Jesus had to wake them several times. His closest friends weren't there for Him in His most desperate time of need. Has that ever happened to you? Jesus understands.

The disciples witnessed miracles and were with Jesus 24/7, yet they still failed. This is a reminder that we all fail and fall short. It's also a reminder that we'll fail people as well. The good news about the cross is that, while many believe the Christian life is about our commitment to God, the cross demonstrates that it's rather about God's commitment to man. It's about His love commitment to us to save us and set us free.

Jesus prayed three times at the Garden of Gethsemane to have the cup of suffering removed, but above all, He wanted to do His Father's will. God had faith in His Son to follow through with His mission to set us free. And, God has faith in you to overcome in your life because Jesus overcame for you and lives in you.

Jesus was tempted to give up. We get tempted to give up, too. Don't beat yourself up for wanting to quit. Remember that God has faith in you, and as a believer, you have all the power of Jesus inside you to overcome any giant or obstacle that comes your way. Declare aloud right now, "My heavenly Father has faith that I can do it!"

> **Luke 22:44, KJV**—"And being in **agony** he prayed more earnestly: and his sweat was as it were great drops of blood falling down to the ground." (emphasis mine)

> **Luke 22:44, AMP**—"And being in **agony** [deeply distressed and anguished; almost to the point of death], He

prayed more intently; and His sweat became like drops of blood, falling down on the ground." (emphasis mine)

The Greek word for *agony* in this verse is the only place where it's used in the *King James Version* of the Bible.

Jesus knew He was about to endure not only excruciating physical pain and torture as a man, but He'd be the only one in the universe to carry the sins of the entire world upon Himself at the cross. I can't imagine the battle and temptations that were going through His mind. Even though it doesn't compare, it reminded me of the tormenting thoughts that I had for years when I was going through bipolar disorder. Jesus understands more than we know.

Jesus' thoughts took a toll on Him, which caused physical exhaustion. Not only that, but He didn't sleep all night. The only place in the Bible where it mentions Jesus sweating drops of blood is in the Gospel of Luke because Luke was a doctor, and this would have stood out to him.

Sweating drops of blood is actually a medical condition called hematidrosis. Merriam-Webster's definition of *hematidrosis* is "the excretion through the skin of blood or blood pigments."[2] There are documented cases of people captured during the world wars, who bled to death in front of the enemy soldiers due to extreme shock or stress. Jesus understands such distress.

The tremendous mental anguish of sweating drops of blood would've drained strength from Jesus' human body even before He endured all the upcoming torment of the cross.

Dr. Zugibe describes what sweating drops of blood does to the body:

> "Jesus' heart pounded against his chest, a cold sweat appeared on His now pale skin, His pupils became dilated, His muscles tightened, and He began to tremble throughout the night. The fact that Jesus 'fell on the ground, and prayed...' (Mark 14:35) was indicative of His weakness because it was unusual for a Jew to kneel during prayer."[3]

Jesus knows what it's like to endure mental anguish! Yet, He had a Father who sent angels to strengthen Him (Luke 22:43) in His time of need, helping Him to overcome, so that one day He could come live in us (those that receive Him), allowing us to also overcome in life. The Father strengthened Jesus, and He'll help you as well.

> **Philippians 4:13, TPT**—"And I find that the strength of Christ's explosive power infuses me to conquer every difficulty."

Tell yourself, "Jesus has got this! He's helping me because I'm His child. I am an overcomer!"

Jesus Understands Betrayal

Have you ever been betrayed, rejected, or abandoned by your closest friends? Unfortunately, it's usually those closest to us who hurt us most. Jesus understands what it's like to be betrayed and rejected by man.

Psalm 22:11, TPT—"So don't leave me now; stay close to me! For trouble is all around me and there's no one else to help me."

Matthew 26:56, TPT—"At that point all of his disciples ran away and abandoned him."

All of the chief priests and elders came with swords and clubs and arrested Jesus after He was betrayed by Judas—a friend and disciple who had spent much time with Him. All of Jesus' friends abandoned Him in His time of need. Peter denied Him three times when asked if he was with Jesus. Jesus knew all of this would happen, yet He still loved Judas and Peter. He knew that He was heading to the cross, which would set people free.

It touches my heart to know that after Jesus rose from the dead, He asked Peter three times if he loved Him. He knew the guilt Peter was undoubtedly carrying because he felt as though he had failed the Lord. God is a restorer, not a condemner. He wants us to receive His love and forgiveness instead of condemnation and guilt.

Additionally, because Jesus lives in believers, we'll never be alone. That's a promise He made to us. When you fail or feel alone, remember this verse and receive it into your heart:

Hebrews 13:5, AMP—"...for He has said, 'I WILL NEVER [under any circumstances] DESERT YOU [nor give you up nor leave you without support, nor will I in any degree leave you helpless], NOR WILL I FORSAKE *or* LET YOU DOWN *or* RELAX MY HOLD ON YOU [assuredly not]!'"

Jesus Understands False Accusations

Have you ever been humiliated or made fun of or falsely accused? It's very painful, but because Jesus understands, He'll get us through the pain. I believe He'll also vindicate us where truth needs to be revealed. I've seen that in my own life concerning false accusations. In some instances, I tried to defend myself, but in others, I let Jesus do it. I believe He leads us as to whether or not we should say anything. But, either way, I've learned that my good, heavenly Father is my defender. He's yours too!

We can talk with Jesus openly about any betrayal, humiliation, or false accusation because He understands and wants to remind us that He'll always take care of us and our situation in accordance with His will. He's a good Daddy, who, at this very moment is working out only good in our life (Romans 8:28).

After He was arrested, Jesus was taken to the Sanhedrin (a Jewish judicial body), where He was questioned, slapped, punched in the face, spit on, and mocked. They blindfolded Him and told Him to prophesy as to who hit Him. They accused Jesus of blasphemy because He said He was the Son of God. He was persecuted for speaking truth. Have you ever been persecuted for speaking truth? I know I have.

Jesus was then sent to Pilate, then to Herod, and then back to Pilate. Injustices took place during the trial. Herod and Pilate found Him not guilty, and the witnesses couldn't come to an agreement as to what should be done with Jesus. It was customary at the time to release a Jewish prisoner before the Passover, so Pilate gave the crowd a choice to release Jesus or a convicted murderer named Barabbas. The crowd chose to release Barabbas and crucify Jesus.

The name *Barabbas* means "Son of a Father"[4] versus the name *Jesus*, which means "Son of God." Some say that Jesus being crucified instead of Barabbas symbolizes that, even though we were guilty, Jesus set us free. Jesus took all sin and punishment for sin. He took our place, just as He took Barabbas', and we go free. That's amazing love!

Jesus Understands Excruciating Pain

Have you experienced physical pain to the point where you felt you couldn't go on? Jesus knows the feeling.

> **Isaiah 53:5, AMP**—"But He was wounded for our transgressions, He was crushed for our wickedness [our sin, our injustice, our wrongdoing]; the punishment [required] for our well-being *fell* on Him, and by His stripes (wounds) we are healed."

Jesus completely paid the price for our healing.

> **Isaiah 50:6, NIV**—"I offered my back to those who beat me, my cheeks to those who pulled out my beard; I did not hide my face from mocking and spitting."

This verse doesn't indicate that Jesus was forced. He *offered* His back. He offered His body as a sacrifice so we could be healed and whole. Why? Because of His passionate love for us.

Isaiah 52:14, NLT—"But many were amazed when they saw him. His face was so disfigured he seemed hardly human, and from his appearance, one would scarcely know he was a man."

During this time, the Roman scourging was the most feared and brutal form of punishment. The Romans made sure their victims experienced the highest degree of pain possible. Many died during a scourging and never made it to their crucifixion. Crucifixion wasn't unusual at this time, but Jesus was the only one who took on the sins and sicknesses of the entire world. He saved humanity by going to the cross.

During a scourging, the Romans used a flagellum, which was a whip with small fragments of animal bones and sharp metal pieces attached to leather strands. Before beginning, the Romans stripped Jesus naked then tied His hands to a post, which He faced, so that His entire back was exposed. Each lash of the flagellum dug into Jesus' flesh, ripping blood vessels, nerves, and skin. Those scourging Jesus took the whip and threw it onto His chest as He stood with His back to His tormentors, so the bone and metal pieces stuck in His skin. Then the whip was pulled toward His back, tearing everything attached to it.

The same process was then applied to His legs and arms, while Jesus most likely cried out in excruciating pain and fell to the ground in agony. Each time He fell, they'd pick Him up to endure more torture. During the scourging, Jesus would've probably experienced tremors, vomiting, and cold sweat due to the trauma. He also had bruises, welts, cuts, and swelling over His entire body.

In *The Crucifixion of Jesus*, Zugibe explains what Jesus would've likely experienced following the brutal scourging:

> "The victim would be reduced to an exhausted, mangled mass of flesh with a craving for water. The scourging propelled Jesus into an early stage of shock. Over the next few hours there would be a slow accumulation of fluid (pleural effusion) developing around the lungs, adding to His breathing difficulties. There would also be lacerations of the liver and perhaps the spleen."[5]

Yet, I'm imagining that with each lash, Jesus thought, *This is so My children can be free. This is so My children can be healed and whole. This is so My children can be righteous and free from emotional torment, betrayal, rejection, shame, and guilt. This is so My children can live a life without condemnation and with freedom.*

If you ever question God's love for you, I encourage you to think about the cross. If you ever question His will for you to walk in healing, look at the cross. See the stripes on His back all because He passionately loves you.

Years ago, I was a self-injurer. I hated myself and thought I was a failure due to the many lies I believed. I thought I needed to punish myself by self-harming. And, it was easier for me to deal with the physical pain than the emotional pain. The voice of condemnation will tell us that we need to pay for our sin or failure, but the cross of Jesus proves that He already paid the price.

One day, in the midst of extreme bondage, while I was cutting my wrist and watching the blood flow, I surprisingly heard the voice of our loving, heavenly Father tell me, "You don't have to do that anymore because My Son shed His blood for you." (You can read my complete story in *Hold On to Hope*.) That was a powerful moment I'll never forget.

Jesus wanted me to know that His blood that He shed on the cross had already set me free from everything that was coming against me: sin, sickness, condemnation, self-injury—everything! Like me, you are forgiven, loved, and accepted, even in the midst of your failures. Jesus doesn't want us holding on to guilt and shame and condemnation. Rather, He wants us to hold on to truth and true freedom that comes only from Him.

The Crown of Thorns

After the scourging, Jesus had difficulty with every step. He was in terrible pain and out of breath. His whole body throbbed. The Romans put a royal scarlet robe on Jesus to mock Him, but He didn't defend Himself. He was on a mission. He had you and me on His mind! His mission was to rescue us, set us free, and come and live His life through us. He even had the people crucifying Him on His mind. He only viewed them with eyes of love, knowing they had no idea what they were doing and that they didn't know the truth that would set them free.

The soldiers put a crown of thorns on Jesus. It's thought that this crown of thorns most likely covered His entire scalp. The thorns were one to two inches long and extremely sharp. Then, they put a staff in His hand and beat Him repeatedly on the head with it, mocking Him and declaring, "Hail! King of the Jews!" Each beating from the staff drove the thorns into His scalp and forehead, causing severe bleeding and pain.

We definitely have nerve endings on the top of our head, which can be demonstrated by tapping the point of a pin on our head. We can only imagine the immense pain Jesus must have felt when these thorns penetrated His scalp and made their way into His nerve endings. The blood that poured from His precious scalp was the same blood that forgives our sins. Jesus willingly became our sacrifice that completely took away our sin, sickness, shame, guilt, condemnation, and death forever.

> **Matthew 27:30, TPT**—"Then they spat in his face and took the reed staff from his hand and hit him repeatedly on his head, driving the crown of thorns deep into his brow."

Dr. Zugibe writes:

> "The blows from the reed [staff] across Jesus' face or against the thorns would have directly irritated the nerves or activated trigger zones across the lip, side of the nose, or face, bringing on severe pains resembling a hot poker or electric shock. The pain would have lancinated across the sides of His face or deep into His ears. …The pain may have stopped almost abruptly, only to recur [after] the slightest movement of the jaws or even from a wisp of wind. Exacerbations and remissions of

throbbing bolts of pain would have occurred all the way to Calvary and during the crucifixion, activated by the movements of walking, falling, and twisting; from the pressure of the thorns across the cross; and from the many shoves and blows by the soldiers."[6]

Take a moment and meditate on this picture of Jesus' suffering, and thank Him from your heart for going to the cross to set you completely free in every area of your life. He had you on His mind while He was being beaten. He had you on His mind when He knew that your sin would be defeated forever. He took the beating on His head so you could have the mind of Christ and peace of mind. Mental illness has no power over any of us because of what Jesus did for us.

The scarlet robe and crown of thorns that Jesus wore symbolized Him taking away our sins and the curse that came with the fall of man, respectively. As seen in Genesis 3:17–18 below, when Adam and Eve sinned, part of the resulting curse was for man to work and sweat with thorns and thistles. Jesus literally sweat drops of blood and worked to go to Calvary to undo every curse against man. The crown of thorns symbolized Him taking that curse of thorns to the grave with Him. He undid everything that was against mankind, so we could be free and whole in every area of our lives. He brought us into a place of spiritual rest.

Genesis 3:17–18, NIV—
"[17]...Cursed is the ground because of you [Adam];
　　through painful toil you will eat food from it
　　all the days of your life.

[18]It will produce thorns and thistles for you,
>   and you will eat the plants of the field."
(brackets mine)

Jesus became the curse for us. We're no longer under the curse of the Law!

> **Galatians 3:13, NLT**—"But Christ has rescued us from the curse pronounced by the law. When he was hung on the cross, he took upon himself the curse for our wrongdoing. For it is written in the Scriptures, 'Cursed is everyone who is hung on a tree.'"

Bible teacher Andrew Wommack believes, as do I, that Jesus was disfigured, not only because of the beating, but because "all the murder, all the perversion, every vile and rotten sin imaginable, all sickness, and all disease ever known to mankind actually entered into His physical human body. ...His body was completely disfigured from cancers, tumors, diseases, deformities and anything else that human beings have ever suffered."[7]

Jesus wore the crown of thorns for us and took the curse so we can wear the crown of glory and take His righteousness! If you're currently struggling with any kind of sickness, imagine that sickness on Jesus' body right now. He took it upon Himself so you can be well. He loves you so much and wants you well more than you do.

The Crucifixion

After Jesus was beaten, His robe was removed and His clothes put back on him. He looked like a mangled mess. I'm certain it was quite painful to put clothes on over His open wounds and exposed muscles and bones. The time had now come for Jesus to be crucified. At this point, He was undoubtedly very weak, lightheaded, sweating, and throbbing in pain; and, He had had nothing to eat.

The soldiers laid a crosspiece across His shoulders. Many scholars don't believe it was an entire cross, but rather a crosspiece, or a long piece of wood, that was tied to Jesus' shoulders. The crosspiece was estimated to have weighed about sixty to seventy-five pounds. Its weight and placement on His open wounds and exposed muscles and nerves caused such pain that it threw Jesus to the ground. Because the crosspiece was tied across His shoulders, there was no way to break His fall when He tumbled to the ground, as He couldn't brace Himself with His arms. Our beautiful Savior endured so much to set us free. This is why He sweated drops of blood in the Garden of Gethsemane. He knew what He was about to endure.

Psalm 22:14–15, TPT—
"14Now I'm completely exhausted; I'm spent.
Every joint of my body has been pulled apart.
My courage has vanished and
my inward parts have melted away.
15 I'm so thirsty and parched—dry as a bone.
My tongue sticks to the roof of my mouth.
And now you've left me in the dust for dead."

The weather was hot and dry, and Jesus was already dehydrated. He was physically exhausted and about to endure the worst part of the crucifixion. He was in a state of traumatic shock, which would've caused Him to be off-balance. As fluid accumulated in His lungs from the scourging, His breathing became problematic. Each time He fell while walking, severe pain shot through His body. There was no way He was going to make the 650-yard journey to Calvary on His own, so they found a man named Simon to carry Jesus' cross the remainder of the way.

I imagine Jesus' breathing difficulties as Him taking all lung conditions and breathing issues upon Himself. He also took all of our panic attacks to the cross and left everything at the grave.

During this time, the streets were busy for the Passover. As Jesus made His way to Calvary, people watched, viewing Him as a criminal deserving of death because criminals were the ones who were crucified. People screamed insults and curses at Him. He was a public spectacle.

The enemy, the devil, thought he had won. He believed that the Messiah was doomed. But the story wasn't over yet. Jesus was about to turn the tables on him, making him the public spectacle.

Colossians 2:14–15, TPT—

"14He canceled out every legal violation we had on our record and the old arrest warrant that stood to indict us. He erased it all—our sins, our stained soul—he deleted it all *and they cannot be retrieved!* Everything we once were in Adam has been placed onto his cross and nailed permanently there as a public display of cancellation.

¹⁵Then Jesus made a public spectacle of all the powers and principalities of darkness, stripping away from them every weapon and all their spiritual authority and power to accuse us. And by the power of the cross, Jesus led them around as prisoners in a procession of triumph. *He was not their prisoner; they were his!"*

Jesus came to Golgotha (Gul-goth-a), a name whose Hebrew origin is akin to "the skull."⁸ His tormentors offered Him a painkiller consisting of wine and myrrh, but Jesus refused it. I believe that Jesus was tempted to take it, but He resisted. Jesus also took all addictions with Him on the cross so we could be free of any such temptation. He overcame so we could overcome with His life and strength living in us.

Jesus understands temptation. If you're tempted with sin, Jesus understands. When the pain of life is so strong that you're tempted to escape in drugs, alcohol, or another addiction, you can draw on the strength of Jesus to overcome. And, if you fail, His love for you never changes. Even on your worst day, your Father says, "I love you. You're beautiful!" Even in your worst failure, your Father says, "I love you. You're beautiful!"

You're safe with Him. Receive His radical love, and it'll cause any addiction to fall away. He'll love you to freedom because He absolutely cherishes you.

Hebrews 2:14–18, TPT—
"¹⁴Since all his 'children' have flesh and blood, so Jesus became human to fully identify with us. He did this, so that he could experience death and annihilate the effects

of the intimidating accuser who holds against us the power of death. [15]By embracing death Jesus sets free those who live their entire lives in bondage to the tormenting dread of death. [16]For it is clear that he didn't do this for the angels, but for all the sons and daughters of Abraham. [17]This is why he had to be a Man and take hold of our humanity in every way. He made us his brothers and sisters and became our merciful and faithful King-Priest before God; as the One who removed our sins to make us one with him. [18]He suffered and endured every test and temptation, so that he can help us every time we pass through the ordeals of life."

John 16:33, AMPC—"I have told you these things, so that in Me you may have [perfect] peace *and* confidence. In the world you have tribulation *and* trials *and* distress *and* frustration; but be of good cheer [take courage; be confident, certain, undaunted]! For I have overcome the world. [I have deprived it of power to harm you and have conquered it for you.]"

After Jesus arrived in Golgotha, the time had come for the final part of His crucifixion—the most painful part. At Golgotha, Jesus was laid on the cross, on the ground. Another man was laid across Jesus' chest to hold Him down. Imagine the pain on His open wounds as the weight of a man rested on top of them.

Nails approximately seven inches long and nearly one-half inch in diameter were driven into Jesus' wrists and His median nerve. Injury to the median nerve is documented as one of the worst pains known to man. Soldiers who experienced shrapnel wounds to the median nerve during World War I often went into shock if the pain was not immediately relieved. The pain is described as unbearable and burning like a lightning bolt traveling across the arm. Jesus experienced this pain with both wrists and then His feet.

Next, soldiers rolled dice for His clothes, with the winner ripping His garments from His body. I'm sure that Jesus' clothes must've been stuck to His body due to all of the dried blood from His wounds and exposed muscles. When His clothes were torn off, it likely felt like His entire body was on fire. The whole cross experience was physically torturous for Jesus, but inside, I know He rejoiced, realizing that His mission would save those who would one day receive this act of love. Jesus couldn't imagine being away from us for all of eternity.

> **Hebrews 12:2, TPT**—"We look away from the natural realm and we fasten our gaze onto Jesus who birthed faith within us and who leads us forward into faith's perfection. His example is this: Because his heart was focused on the joy of knowing that you would be his, he endured the agony of the cross and conquered its humiliation, and now sits exalted at the right hand of the throne of God!"

What the Cross Bought

Jesus was in agony on the cross, experiencing the weight of the sins of the entire world upon Himself. And, having difficulty breathing, especially with the position in which He had been nailed onto the cross, He cried out, "My God, My God, why have you deserted me?" (Matthew 27:46, TPT).

This is the only time Jesus ever referred to God as "My God" instead of "My Father." In that moment, Jesus was experiencing the sins of sexual abuse, murder, anger, and every other evil sin imaginable. Jesus took all punishment and wrath for sin so we could be completely free and reconciled to our good Father, which was always God's desire. Our Father knew that mankind had a corrupted view of Him, but He wanted us to know through Jesus' death on the cross that He never changed His mind or His love for His people. Man was the one who needed to change his mind about how God saw him and His love toward him.

The Father never stopped loving mankind and never will. He can't because He is love. In fact, Ephesians 1:4–5 says that He chose us and loved us before the foundation of the world. He loved us before we ever sinned. Jesus died while we were yet sinners to show us His love even while we were considered sinners (Romans 5:8). His love for us is relentless! Knowing what Jesus did for us on the cross should cause us to effortlessly fall deeper in love with Him.

God's plan of redemption was now being fulfilled, and I'm sure heaven rejoiced the moment Jesus was resurrected from the grave three days after He gave up His spirit on the cross. God is not mad at us. Declare right now, "God is never mad at me! He loves me!"

Isaiah 54:9, NLT—"Just as I swore in the time of Noah that I would never again let a flood cover the earth, so now I swear that I will never again be angry and punish you."

Jesus cried out, "It is finished!" (John 19:30, NKJV). He knew He had conquered everything that was against us. He understood that we would be recipients of the new covenant He made with His Father on our behalf that can never be broken. God cannot fail. That's good news! By bringing us into the new covenant, He rendered the old obsolete. He knew that sin would no longer have power over us and that by His stripes, healing was ours to receive. We were no longer under the curse of the Law! You can read the curses in Deuteronomy 28 and know that those do not belong to us because of Jesus.

Jesus destroyed the works of the devil so that he has no power over us. He conquered death. We are free! When Jesus rose again, we rose with Him, and we are now seated in heavenly places in a position of victory, not defeat. We are winners in the kingdom!

There are many beautiful benefits Jesus gave us by enduring the cross. All we need to do is just simply receive them and say, "Thank You!"

Through the cross…

We became new creations (2 Corinthians 5:17)

Jesus bore our sin and gave us the gift of righteousness (Romans 5:17; 1 Peter 2:24)

Jesus provided physical and emotional healing (Isaiah 53:5)

Jesus brought us into a secure covenant with better promises that can never be altered (Hebrews 8:6–7)

Jesus gave us His life (Romans 8:10–11)

Jesus understands our temptations (Hebrews 4:15–16)

Jesus understands betrayal, trauma, rejection, false accusations, and pain (Matthew 26:14–16; 27:27–50; Mark 6:1–6; 14:34; 15:55–65)

To receive these benefits, believe what Jesus has provided on the cross for you, and declare:

I am loved!

I am forgiven!

I am righteous!

I am secure in God's love!

I am a cherished child of God!

If you're able to take communion, I encourage you to do so after learning all that Jesus provided for you on the cross. Thank Him and remind yourself of the many benefits of His finished work. Communion is a powerful tool toward healing.

CHAPTER 2

NO CONDEMNATION!
THE CASE IS CLOSED!

Imagine if a young boy asks his father, "Daddy, can you teach me how to ride a bike?" The father gets a frown on his face, annoyed that his son is bothering him. But then he thinks, *If I teach him how to ride a bike, maybe he'll stay out of my way.*

"I guess I can teach you," he says in an unemotional tone. "Put your hands on the handle bars. I'm going to push you, and you'll need to look straight ahead and keep pedaling." His son, Sam, has fear in his eyes, which annoys his father even more. Sam doesn't seem ready and would like his father to explain more to him, but he's afraid to ask. His father grows increasingly impatient.

Suddenly, Sam's father pushes him on the bike after walking alongside him for a few steps. Sam pedals about a foot before falling off the bike. His father approaches him angrily and points his finger at him, saying, "I told you to keep pedaling and keep going, but you didn't listen to me. Can't you do anything right? You messed up. You never listen to me."

Sam looks at his father, regretting ever asking him for help. He vows to never ask him for anything again and to certainly not go to him when he makes a mistake. Heartbroken and afraid, Sam no longer trusts his father. He just wants to run away and hide.

Now, imagine a different scenario where Sam asks his father, "Daddy, can you teach me how to ride a bike?" This time, his father gets a huge smile on his face and replies, "I would love to teach you how to ride a bike. In fact, I've been waiting for this moment!"

Sam's father takes quite a bit of time explaining to him how to ride. He's obviously very involved in Sam's life, and it brings him great joy to spend time teaching his son something new. Even though Sam is nervous, he's motivated to learn because his father is so excited, and he trusts that his father can help him.

The father starts walking and then running with his son, as they both excitedly wait to see what happens. The father lets go and shouts, "You can do it, Sam! I know you can do it!" Sam continues pedaling on his own for about five feet, but then starts to lose his balance and falls. The father immediately runs to him and asks, "Are you okay?" In a shaky voice, Sam responds, "Yes, Daddy, but I have a scrape on my knee." His father helps Sam to his feet, kisses his scrape, and says, "I'm so proud of you for trying! I'm going to help you. I know you can do this. You're amazing!"

His father's words motivate Sam to try again, and on the third try, he successfully rides his bike. Father and son hug and rejoice together, even though Sam failed a couple of times before succeeding.

Which of these two scenarios represents a good father? How would the condemning father in the first scenario cause you to react? Would you want to go to him when you failed, or would you want to hide from him? Could his condemnation maybe cause you to live in a place of fear of failure, leading to perfectionism?

Unfortunately, many people believe that our heavenly Father condemns them or gets mad when they fail. Oftentimes, we take the experiences that we've had with our earthly father and project them onto our heavenly Father, thinking He must be the same way, yet nothing could be further from the truth.

Trauma and Fear

I grew up with a condemning father. I constantly lived in fear, especially fear of failure. He used fear as a tactic to get his children to obey him. Once, when I was about eight, my father and step-mother took me to our neighbor's, who had an infant about seven months old. My parents and neighbors may have been smoking marijuana or doing an exchange of marijuana, which they frequently did. The baby and I were playing nearby with her toys, which were strewn across the floor.

Suddenly, the parents asked, "Is she choking?" Apparently, the baby put one of her toys in her mouth and was choking, but I had no idea that was happening because I knew nothing about taking care of babies. My father stood, and I remember the feeling I had looking up at him. The raging look on his face said to me, "I'm going to kill you if something happens to this baby. It's all your fault she's choking because you were playing with her."

I was traumatized. The parents were able to take the toy out of her mouth, and all was well. They didn't blame me for anything. They knew I was playing with the baby in her own home with her toys. Yet, I felt shame and humiliation and fear from my father, who never did apologize to me. This was one of many examples that caused me to constantly walk on eggshells and live a childhood filled with fear and fear of failure. This led to believing that I had to always be perfect, which is impossible. It also affected my future relationships, as I viewed life through the lens of rejection and fear. It's not a fun way to live!

When I became born again at the age of ten, I projected some of that fear onto my heavenly Father. I thought He was out to get me every time I failed, just like my British grandmother who'd whack my sister and me with a wooden spoon whenever we'd do something wrong. I thought God had a giant wooden spoon and was just waiting to whack me with it.

My beliefs were all lies because our good, amazing, loving heavenly Father will never condemn us, especially when we fail. He's like the Father in the second scenario, not the first. It's imperative to understand this because as long as we're in our natural body, we'll continue to fail and fall short.

No Condemnation!

Romans 8:1, TPT—"*So now the case is closed.* There remains no accusing voice of condemnation against those who are joined in life-union with Jesus, the Anointed One."

One definition of *condemnation* is "the expression of strong disapproval, pronouncing to be wrong."[1] Synonyms of *condemnation* include *criticism* and *rebuke*.[2]

The Greek word for *condemnation* is *katakrino*, which means "to give judgment against, worthy of punishment."[3] The root word of *condemnation* is *katakrima*, meaning "penalty."[4]

Let's look at Romans 8:1 again in *The Passion Translation* with emphasis based on the definitions above:

"*So now the case is closed.* There remains no accusing voice of condemnation (disapproval, criticism, rebuke; God will never disapprove of you, criticize you, or rebuke you; He'll never hold judgment against you or penalize you) against those who are joined in life-union with Jesus, the Anointed One."

I encourage you to declare aloud, "So now the case is closed! There remains no accusing voice of condemnation, disapproval, criticism, or rebuke. God will never disapprove of me, criticize me, or rebuke me. He'll never hold judgment against me or penalize me because I'm joined in life-union with Jesus, the Anointed One."

That should make you want to do a happy dance! God is rejoicing with you! Everything discussed in Chapter 1 pertaining to Jesus on the cross is the reason for this good news.

Additionally, an antonym of *condemnation* is *approval*.[5] Substituting this into Romans 8:1, the verse now reads:

"So now the case is closed! There remains only approval for those who are joined in life-union with Jesus, the Anointed One."

The gospel is good news! The cross made a difference. It's important to read the Bible through new covenant lenses. Everything in the Bible was written *for* us, but not everything was written *to* us. We now live in a new covenant, and Jesus has taken care of our sin issue. We no longer have to offer sacrifices for sin or worry about plucking out our eyes if they cause us to sin: "And if your eye causes you to stumble, gouge it out and throw it away. It is better for you to enter life with one eye than to have two eyes and be thrown into the fire of hell" (Matthew 18:9, NIV).

As a little girl, I was so scared when I read this passage because I didn't understand how to read the Bible through new covenant lenses. Now I know that Jesus has taken care of sin, and God views us with a clean slate, as if we've never sinned. He's a good Father who is not mad at us, doesn't condemn us, and pursues us with His love and grace when we fail.

Another translation of the full verse of Romans 8:1 reads: "There is therefore now no condemnation to them which are in Christ Jesus, **who walk not after the flesh, but after the Spirit**" (KJV, emphasis mine). This second half of the verse (in bold) was not in the oldest and most reliable manuscripts and was added by the translators.[6]

Perhaps the translators thought this was too-good-to-be-true news, but it is true! The good news is that the gospel is not based on us and our behavior, but it's based on Jesus and His finished work. We receive Jesus' finished work as a loving gift so we can live a life of joy, peace, and freedom. We need to hold on to this truth.

> **Romans 8:1, AMP**—"Therefore there is now no condemnation [no guilty verdict, no punishment] for those who are in Christ Jesus [who believe in Him as personal Lord and Savior]."

The definition of the word *no* is "a negative used to express dissent,"[7] with the following synonym phrases: *not in any degree, way, or under any condition; by no means, in no wise, none,* and *never.*[8]

Inserting these synonyms into Romans 8:1 for emphasis, it reads: "Therefore there is now not in any degree, way, or under any condition; by no means, in no wise, none, never any disapproval, criticism, rebuke, judgment against, or penalty for those who are in Christ Jesus."

Our part is to receive this and say, "Thank You," to our beautiful, perfect, amazing, and loving Savior, Jesus, who took the sin of the entire world and removed all condemnation from us.

Sins Removed

> **Hebrews 8:12, AMP**—"I will be merciful and gracious toward their wickedness, and I will remember their sins no more."

> **Psalm 103:12, AMP**—"As far as the east is from the west, so far has He removed our transgressions from us."

Geography has never been my strong suit. In fact, since there is no condemnation, I'll share with you that when I was invited to speak in Thailand several years ago, I had to research where it was! I do know, however, how to calculate how far the east is from the west, and I know that they can never touch. Our sins have been removed thanks to Jesus. We are forgiven and loved.

I encourage you to meditate on this. Once this becomes truth rooted deep in your heart, you'll feel loved and safe with the Lord, even when you fail. Sometimes I forget this truth and have to remind myself. I remind myself that I'm loved, forgiven, safe, and cherished by my good Father at all times, even when I fail. Our behavior doesn't change our position or right standing with Him. Everything in the world tells us, "If you do bad, you'll get bad back, and if you do good, you'll get good back." This is the world's system.

But the gospel says that even when we do bad, we're still right with God. It's not that your behavior is always right, but you remain in right standing with the Father. He views you as good, not bad. You are His treasured child, and He knows that when you understand your forgiveness and righteousness, you will live holy effortlessly. You will no longer want to sin and fail. But, when you do—as we all do—you will run to His throne of grace for Him to love you and help you in your time of need. He's the Daddy of our dreams!

White as Snow

Isaiah 1:18, AMP—"'Come now, and let us reason together,' says the LORD. 'Though your sins are like scarlet, they shall be as white as snow; Though they are red like crimson, They shall be like wool.'"

Imagine having a red piece of paper, which symbolizes sin. Then, place a piece of white paper completely over the red paper. Cover it entirely so no red can be seen. It's white like snow. That's exactly what Jesus did, except He didn't just cover our sins; He removed them.

Although the white paper represents our identity in Christ, many in the body of Christ feel a mixture of both. They believe that they're righteous and forgiven—until they fail. The voice of accusation tells righteous believers that they need to pay for their sin by feeling extreme guilt and shame, even though Jesus says, "I made you as white as snow. I don't even remember your sins anymore, and they're completely removed as far as the east is from the west."

When we choose to carry guilt and forget our forgiveness, we walk around like a "pink" Christian instead of a "white-as-snow" one. It's as if we mixed the red and white papers and are now viewing ourselves as pink. If you start to forget who you are after you fail, remember the red and white papers and how the Father always sees you as white as snow.

Knowing our identity in Christ and His forgiveness allows us to admit when we're wrong and to apologize. I've heard people use the excuse of being forgiven to never admit they're wrong. That's because pride has taken root. Knowing our identity allows us to say we're sorry and right the wrongs. I also know that when I fail and go to my heavenly Father, I'm already forgiven. But since we have a relationship, I tell Him that I'm sorry I messed up. He loves on me, reminds me of who I am, and gives me wisdom of what to do or the grace to get through any relational or earthly consequence.

Knowing our identity also allows us to walk in righteousness and peace instead of shame and condemnation. I lived in a constant state of condemnation for many years due to relapsing on alcohol, cutting myself, and going to psych wards, among other things. I can say with certainty that even if you're in the midst of any of these in your own life, there's no condemnation for you. The Father wants to fill the love void in your life so you can walk in healing and wholeness.

God doesn't condemn us, but people do. There's an enemy that wants to steal, kill, and destroy, and he does that through people in order to ruin our relationships. We have a real enemy, but that enemy isn't other people. We can't afford to receive the condemning words thrown against us by others. God wants us to remember our worth and value in Him. The enemy will try to get us entangled in depression, sadness, anxiety, and frustration. He'll also try to make us think there's something wrong with us and that we'll never get it right.

This is why it's life changing to know the truth of our identity: who God says we are and who He says He is. This will allow us to hold on to freedom. We must stand against those negative voices and refuse for them to take root in our hearts. However, even if we do receive them, as I know I have, we can repent, or change our mind, and go back to the truth. We can do this at any moment, even right now. There's no condemnation for you, even when you fail to believe the truth. There's only love for you from our heavenly Father, and He'll remind you that you're amazing and beautiful—the child He always dreamed of having. You are His dream come true!

When we live with a righteousness consciousness instead of a sin consciousness, we live in peace. It causes joy to bubble up, and it's a contagious joy to others. I believe this is a huge key to escaping depression. I know this to be true because it happened in my own life. Your identity is not a depressed, mentally ill person with addictions. It's simply a precious, loved, and cherished child of God.

The Case Is Closed!

When a judge hammers the gavel, it means the case is closed. The evidence has been presented, and a decision has been made. I believe I've presented enough evidence from the Word of God to prove that there's no condemnation for you, only love. When the voice of accusation comes, imagine Jesus taking that gavel, slamming it down, and saying, "The case is closed! It is finished! My blood has set you free!"

Now, when you hear:

"You said you were going to exercise today, but you didn't. You're a loser."

"You ate too much chocolate today. You're a big failure."

"You yelled at your kids. You're a horrible mother."

"You just called the driver who cut you off an idiot. Some Bible college graduate example you are!"

"You teach on healing, yet you're sick. You must be a defective Christian."

"You only got two 'Amens!' when you spoke, but the other speaker got ten. You're a terrible speaker. You should just quit ministry."

The list goes on and on. Which voices of accusation come at you? They'll be different for everyone depending on our life experiences. When those voices come, remind yourself that you're not a failure, you're not a loser, you're not a defective Christian, and you're not a terrible speaker or a horrible parent. Remind yourself of the truth of your identity. Your identity is not your behavior. Your identity is based on how your Father sees you, and He sees you as flawless in His sight because of the blood of Jesus.

Jesus said in John 8:32 that knowing the truth sets us free. If truth sets us free, then what keeps us in bondage? Lies. We need to replace those lies with the truth and meditate on it instead. Maybe you believe that your life is a mess and that you made some bad decisions. You may wonder why God would want to help you out of your mess instead of condemning you or getting mad at you. Maybe your old negative childhood mindsets tell you that God's not happy with you and you're not accepted. If that's the case, the following verse will give you peace:

Psalm 34:17–18, AMP—"When the righteous cry [for help], the LORD hears and rescues them from all their distress and troubles. The LORD is near to the heartbroken...."

If you believe in Jesus and what He did for you, God calls you righteous. When you cry for help, your good Father will rescue you from all of your troubles, not just some of them. Scripture doesn't say that He'll only deliver you from those troubles that you didn't get yourself into. There's no prerequisite for Him helping you. He rescues you because He's a loving and rescuing Father, and you are His precious child. Period.

Being abused as a child caused me to immediately receive voices of condemnation, which told me I was unworthy, defective, dirty, and on and on. I eventually turned to self-injury and addictions. Eventually, I was diagnosed with many mental illnesses and addictions, which I received into my life because I didn't know who I was in Christ or what Jesus did for me to set me free. I carried the labels of "outcast," "mentally ill," "crazy," a "piece of junk," and "there is definitely something wrong with me."

I couldn't look people in the eyes because I was filled with shame. I never felt good enough. I didn't measure up to others' standards, even my own.

Proverbs 23:7 had become a reality in my life:

Proverbs 23:7, KJV—"For as he thinketh in his heart, so is he."

Even though all of those labels and voices of condemnation I received for my heart weren't my truth, because I believed they were *the* truth, my behavior was consistent with a bipolar, defective, crazy, shame-filled woman with addictions.

This is why truth sets us free. When we believe that we're righteous, beautiful, loved, forgiven, and precious children of God, we'll act accordingly. It's not difficult, but it's a process of renewing our mind to God's Word. But, our heavenly Father helps us get there. Don't hesitate to ask Him for help.

Claude's Epiphany

After my husband unexpectedly had triple-bypass surgery several years ago, the nurse wanted him to start walking the next day. I understand that it sounds a bit scary to think about that. One nurse in particular showed Claude some "tough love." He didn't care for this nurse and wanted to submit a complaint about her. Nonetheless, he began walking, and I went with him as he walked the hallway. He'd slowly take one excruciating step at a time, breathing heavily in and out with each one. He didn't get very far on his walks, but we both thought that was normal given the fact that he just had his chest completely cut open and his heart taken out and repaired during an hours-long surgery.

But Claude's "favorite" nurse asked him, "Why are you walking like an old man?" Claude was only forty-six years young at the time of his surgery! He responded, "You mean I can walk normally? I don't have to walk this slowly?"

She said, "Absolutely not! You can walk normally, and you should." Claude had an instant shift in his thinking and started walking normally from that point on. He even ended up thanking this nurse at the end of his stay and giving her an amazing review. That makes me laugh! This is a true example of how our beliefs affect our behavior. It also demonstrates why it's good for us to encourage others and tell them, "You can do it!"

The Father's Good Thoughts about You

We must begin to have a hatred for the voices of condemnation. Condemnation cannot reside where truth lives. Truth trumps condemnation. We need to view condemnation like a squatter who tries to take illegal residence in our mind and temple and tell it to get lost, just as we would an intruder.

Not only does God not condemn us, but He never has any condemning thoughts about us, even when we mess up. Meditate on the following verses from *The Passion Translation*. This is how your good Father views you:

> **Psalm 139:17**—"Every single moment you are thinking of me. How precious and wonderful to consider that you cherish me constantly in your every thought."

> **Psalm 40:5**—"...And you think of us all the time, thinking of us all the time with your countless expressions of love—far exceeding our expectations!"

It's a joy for our Father to think good thoughts about us. It's not burdensome for Him as it is for us sometimes to think well of others. It's an effortless joy. He is pure love. You're on His mind right now, and He's thinking about how awesome you are and how much He loves you.

When you're found "not guilty" in a court, it means that you're free from the charge of an offense, as far as the criminal law is concerned. Under the rules of double jeopardy, you can never be charged with that crime again. If God were to punish you or remember your sins, He would be unjust. It would be considered double jeopardy to punish the same sin twice. God is just, and you can trust that He is because He made you righteous. He is just because He never condemns you. And, He is just because He never gets mad at you. The price was paid by Jesus. You are loved, accepted, righteous, holy, flawless, and a beautiful, treasured child of God. The case is forever closed!

CHAPTER 3

SAFE IN THE ARMS OF OUR GOOD SHEPHERD

The study of Psalm 23 was one of my favorite times of studying the Bible. This chapter helped me understand our good Father in a deeper way. It's a tender chapter that I believe will show you another glimpse of the Father's love. I touched on some of this in my book, *Hold On to Hope*, but I want to expand on it here. I could hear the truths from this chapter every day and never tire of it. It's so important for us to continually immerse ourselves in the Father's love toward us, which is revealed as we study His Word.

I once heard someone say that worry is when we imagine our future without the goodness of God and when we meditate on how God is going to fail us. Thinking about worry in this manner will get our attention! When I minister and talk about this perspective of worry, I hear gasps from the audience as people realize the depth of truth in these statements.

How do you think your life would change if you never worried about anything ever again? How would your life change if you never again experienced fear in any area of your life?

Our good Father loves us so much. He always wants us to receive revelation of who He is so we can trust Him no matter what comes our way. If we don't believe that He's always good to us, it'll be impossible for us to trust Him, especially in the face of significant trials.

Because some of us have grown up with inconsistent and untrustworthy fathers, we find it difficult to believe—consciously or subconsciously—that God is truly trustworthy. Sometimes we think He needs our help in managing our lives, and we want to remain in control. When we strive to control our lives instead of trusting God in a place of rest, stress and worry enter our heart.

God wants to help us realize without a shadow of a doubt that He's good and has our best interests at heart. When we do, we can trust Him and receive from Him. My prayer for you is that you come to know just how good He really is. And, Psalm 23 is the perfect chapter to begin to understand His love.

Words related to *sheep* or *shepherd* are mentioned in the Bible over 600 times. Obviously, God wanted to communicate something to us! As we dive into this chapter, it's important to remember that it was written from the perspective of a well-cared-for sheep named David. During his life, David encountered many trials. He committed adultery and murder, and King Saul and his army constantly sought to kill him. Yet, David was considered a man after God's own heart.

David understood that even when he failed, he was loved by his good Father. He knew He was forgiven. He didn't run and hide from God; rather, He ran straight into His arms. This psalm reveals the revelation that David had of the Father. Although it was written over 2000 years ago in a culture we're not familiar with, it's still relevant today because it depicts God's timeless love for us.

Knowing Him as Our Best Friend

Psalm 23:1, NIV—"The LORD is my shepherd, I lack nothing."

Psalm 23:1, TPT—"The Lord is my best friend and my shepherd. I always have more than enough."

According to *The Passion Translation Bible*, "The word most commonly used for *shepherd* is taken from the root word *ra'ah*, which is also the Hebrew word for *best friend*."[1]

Using the word *my* is an indication of intimacy. David didn't know God as *a* shepherd, but he knew Him as *my* Shepherd. In the same way, God doesn't want us to know Him as *a* father, but He wants us to know Him as *our* Father. Intimacy also occurs between best friends. A best friend is often described as someone who knows everything about you but still accepts you. Our good Father knows everything about us, yet He loves us and accepts us, and His great desire is to have a relationship with us, His kids.

People will fail us, and we'll fail people. But God is the best friend who'll never betray you, talk bad about you, leave you, or hurt you in any way. He's the only relationship with 100 percent pure motives that we'll ever have in our lives.

He Knows Us Intimately

When a shepherd sees his flock of sheep, he doesn't just see a herd of sheep. He intimately knows each one. He knows the sheep's personalities and the family each comes from. There's intimacy between a good shepherd and his sheep. In the same way, when our heavenly Father sees a crowd of people, He knows each person in the crowd uniquely and individually. He knows the number of hairs on each head, the cares and concerns of every person's heart, the individual traumas that have been overcome, the family that each person belongs to or the pain that was suffered due to abandonment, and every other personal detail about each man and woman.

God is a relational God who knows us intimately. He knows the sound of your voice, the sound of your laugh, the number of tears you've cried, and the good times and bad times you've been through. He's been there all along, even when we didn't know it. He's a good Daddy who never leaves us.

I once read a story of a voice impersonator who attempted to impersonate the voice of a shepherd to see if he could cause the shepherd's sheep to come to him. The impersonator was very good. He listened to the shepherd call his sheep, and his impersonation was nearly an exact duplicate of the shepherd's voice. But the sheep were not fooled; they didn't come to the man. They knew the voice was not that of their shepherd that they had come to know so intimately.

The voice impersonator then asked the shepherd if he could try again, this time wearing the shepherd's clothes. The shepherd agreed, and the man again called the sheep. But, once again, the sheep were not deceived, and they didn't come.

In the same way, the more we grow to intimately know the voice of the Father in our own lives, the more we won't be deceived by the voices of condemnation, shame, guilt, addictions, rejection, or anything else the enemy tries to send us.

We were created to be loved by and in a relationship with a loving Father. The more we know Him, the more we'll depend on Him, and we won't get deceived into following a stranger's voice (John 10:4–5). It was interesting to learn that sheep require more attention and care than any other livestock because they can't take care of themselves. The Bible likens believers to sheep because we were created to depend on our good Father for everything in life.

It's the shepherd's responsibility to care for the sheep, making sure they're safe and sound at all times. The shepherd watches over the sheep continually, and there's no greater reward for the shepherd than to see his sheep thriving and doing well. Likewise, the Father delights in taking care of us. He delights in meeting all our needs and desires. In fact, He provided everything we'd ever need by having Christ live in us.

God doesn't want us to live a life of anxiety and worry but instead depend on Him and involve Him in our everyday lives. He wants us to know that we're in the care of a good Shepherd, who always has our best interests at heart. And, just as sheep are the object of the shepherd's affection, we are the object of the Father's affection. As discussed in Chapter 2, He has good thoughts about us all the time.

He Gives Us Rest

Psalm 23:2a, NIV—"He makes me lie down in green pastures, he leads me beside quiet waters."

The Hebrew words for *lie down* mean "lead them to rest."[2] *Leads me* in Hebrew means "bring to a place of rest."[3] And, *quiet waters* means "waters of rest."[4]

Psalm 23:2a, TPT—"He offers a resting place for me in His luxurious love."

If sheep are hungry, afraid, stressed out, or have strife with the other sheep, they're unable to rest until everything is calm. They can't rest until they feel safe. A shepherd's job is to ensure that his sheep are full, at peace, safe, free from parasites, and rested. The sheep trust a good shepherd to take care of their every need. Without a shepherd, they can't rest. They can't even live!

This is a great analogy for us. We need our good Father for everything. Living life depending on Him for our every need brings peace and joy instead of anxiety and stress. When we try to live life on our own without Him, working and striving to do everything ourselves, it leads to frustration instead of peace.

During the time when Jesus walked the earth, the hills of Bethlehem were not lush and green. The shepherds actually had to work to produce grass for their sheep. They had to clear rocks, tear out stumps and brush, and sometimes burn the dead grass. Then they had to water so a lush patch of grass could grow for the sheep to graze on.

Our good Shepherd makes us lie down in His finished work. When Jesus went to the cross, the stripes on His back, the nails in His hands, and the blood He shed for us were so we could be free and live a life of rest.

Bestselling author Max Lucado writes in his book *Traveling Light*, "When David said, 'He makes me lie down in green pastures,' he's saying, 'My Shepherd makes me lie down in His finished work. With His own pierced hands, Jesus created a pasture for the soul. He tore out the thorny underbrush of condemnation. He pried loose the huge boulders of sin. In their place, He planted seeds of grace and dug ponds of mercy.'"[5]

Hebrews 10:11–13 presents a beautiful depiction of what Jesus did for us: "Every human priest stands day by day performing his religious duties and offering time after time the same sacrifices—which can never actually remove sins. But this man, after offering one sacrifice for sins forever, took his seat at God's right hand, from that time offering no more sacrifice, but waiting until 'his enemies be made his footstool'" (PHILLIPS).

After Jesus became the final sacrifice for sin, He sat to show that His job was finished. Sitting is a place of rest. The Old Testament priests never sat, as they offered sacrifices for sins daily. In fact, in the tabernacle or temple, there were no chairs or places for priests to sit.

Jesus provided complete forgiveness for sins, gave us the gift of righteousness, and came to live inside born-again believers. Because He lives in us, we have everything we need to live this life, and all our needs are met by Him. We can draw on His joy, peace, love, and strength whenever we need it. This is great news! We're not alone, and we were never meant to live life on our own.

How do we know when we're resting in the finished work of Jesus? Peace and rest will be the fruit. If you find yourself in a place of stress and anxiety, take a deep breath, give yourself grace, and meditate on the truths in God's Word. Ask the Father to speak to your heart. Ask Him how He sees you, and He'll speak to you and show you His love. He wants us to depend on Him. Jesus invites us to rest daily in His arms, His promises, and His love. You are always welcomed!

His Still Waters

Jesus declared in John 6:35, "I am the bread of life. Whoever comes to me will never go hungry, and whoever believes in me will never be thirsty" (NIV).

We can lie down and rest like well-cared-for sheep that have been fed and given water because Jesus meets our every need. We can rest in Jesus and in His Word. We can rest in His promises, which are "Yes!" and "Amen!" for us (2 Corinthians 1:20).

Imagine the joy in the heart of our good Father and Shepherd when He sees His sheep — His beloved children — resting in His finished work and resting in Him! He loves to see His sheep thriving and being cared for. His "pasture," or His finished work of defeating sin, healing sickness, removing guilt and shame, and other benefits, is a gift to us. A gift is to be received and doesn't need to be earned. Jesus already paid the price for it. We just say, "Thank You, Jesus! I believe and receive it."

Psalm 23:2b, NIV—"...He leads me beside quiet waters."

Psalm 23:2b, TPT—"His tracks take me to an oasis of peace, the quiet brook of bliss."

Sheep are afraid of rushing waters, and they won't drink from them because of this fear. If only rushing water is available to the sheep, the shepherd will place large rocks in the water, forming a wall that causes the rushing waters to be still and peaceful. What a beautiful picture of a loving shepherd caring for his sheep.

This reminds me of Jesus when He was in the boat with His disciples. They encountered a storm, which produced huge waves. His disciples became afraid, but Jesus rebuked the winds and waves and calmed the storm (Matthew 8:23–27).

Notice that Jesus was in the boat with His disciples, yet a storm still arose. We'll also encounter trials and storms in our lives, but Jesus will be there for us through them all. One of the benefits of His finished work is that He gave us His authority. Mark 11:23 tells us that we can speak to the mountains — or difficulties — in our lives and command them to move out of our way.

Our good Shepherd has given us everything we need to live a victorious life. This is why we must study the Word of God. If we don't know what's ours and what we have in Him, we won't benefit from it. God said in Hosea 4:6 that His "...people are destroyed from lack of knowledge" (NIV). We need to know what Jesus paid the price for us to have so we can live a life of joy and rest no matter what comes our way. We have His resurrection power in us, and when we speak His Word, we have the power to change situations and circumstances.

The Father always leads us into peace. Sheep keep their eyes on their shepherd to know where he's leading them. In the same way, we must keep our eyes on our good Shepherd, who leads and guides us and gives us His wisdom when needed. When we take our eyes off Him, we start to falter, just as Peter did when he took His eyes off Jesus and began to sink (Matthew 14:22–30). If we keep looking at Jesus instead of the storm, we'll stay in peace.

> **Isaiah 26:3, AMP**—"You will keep him in perfect and constant peace the one whose mind is steadfast [that is, committed and focused on You—in both inclination and character], because he trusts and takes refuge in You [with hope and confident expectation]."

The definition of *peace* is "freedom of the mind from annoyance, distraction, anxiety and obsession." It means "tranquility."[6]

With these definitions in mind, Isaiah 26:3 reads: "You will keep him in perfect and constant peace (freedom of the mind from annoyance, distraction, anxiety and obsession; tranquility) the one whose mind is steadfast [that is, committed and focused on You—in both inclination and character], because he trusts and takes refuge in You [with hope and confident expectation]."

Sometimes God leads us into times of rest and stillness, like the quiet waters in Psalm 23. In fact, Psalm 46:10 instructs us to "Be still and know (recognize, understand) that I am God" (AMP).

He may lead us to put our phones away, take a break from social media, or go for a nature walk so we can give Him our full attention. God always speaks to us, but sometimes we can't hear Him clearly due to the many distractions around us.

He knows that when we focus our attention on Him, we'll hear His voice guiding us, laughing with us, comforting us, or loving us. He also knows that we're strengthened when we're quiet in His presence. He loves us and wants us living a life of peace and rest that only comes from knowing Him intimately.

He Restores Us

Psalm 23:3a, NIV—"He refreshes my soul." The Hebrew word for *refreshes* means "brings back."[7]

Psalm 23:3a, TPT—"That's where he restores and revives my life."

Matthew 18:11–12 tells us, "[11]For the Son of man came to save [from the penalty of eternal death] that which was lost. [12]What do you think? If a man has a hundred sheep, and one of them has gone astray and gets lost, will he not leave the ninety-nine on the mountain and go in search of the one that is lost?" (AMPC).

God is a rescuing Father. The Father sending Jesus to rescue us was the ultimate rescue for all of mankind. Yet, He still continues to rescue us in our everyday lives because He's a good Father who loves and cherishes us and wants to help us. He cares about every intimate detail of our lives.

I can just imagine the shepherd looking for that lost sheep, so focused on the mission of bringing it back safe and sound that nothing could stand in His way. A good shepherd won't rest until he finds his lost sheep.

There's something called a cast sheep, which is a sheep that's lying flat on its back with its legs flailing because it can't get up. It may've hit a groove in the ground that caused it to lose its balance and fall over, or it may be pregnant or have fur that's thicker on one side, causing it to become off-balance. A cast sheep is a sheep that's in trouble. It can't get back on its feet and will typically cry out in anxiety. It needs a shepherd to help it.

Shepherds know about cast sheep, so if they realize that one of their sheep has gone missing, they'll leave their flock to search for it. When the shepherd reaches the cast sheep, he'll grab the sheep's legs and put it back on its feet. Sometimes the sheep will initially be unable to walk, so the shepherd will rub its legs to aid in circulation until it can once again walk on its own.

This is a beautiful picture of our loving Father restoring us. When we find ourselves in a mess—even of our own making—full of anxiety, fear, and hopelessness, He'll come and rescue us. He'll reach out His loving arms and help us to our feet, no questions asked. Our good Father doesn't say, "Sorry, I can't help you because you did this to yourself," or, "Sorry, I already rescued you yesterday. You only get one rescue a week." Or, He won't ask, "How much were you in the Word this week?" or, "Why didn't you listen to Me? You never get it right!" Instead, His love says, "My child, I will rescue you as many times as you need rescuing because I am your good Father. Let Me help you out of your mess."

Sometimes we have consequences we must deal with in regards to laws or relationships. Yet, God is a loving Father who helps us every step of the way with whatever we need. Our only response is to allow Him to rescue us. Will we kick Him when He holds His hands out? Will we push Him away, or will we hold on to His rescuing hands and allow Him to pull us to our feet? If we trust a good and loving Father, we'll gladly give our hand to His. If we don't trust Him, we might try to rescue ourselves.

Psalm 91:14–16 from *The Message* Bible beautifully articulates the heart of our rescuing Father:

> "'If you'll hold on to me for dear life,' says GOD,
>   'I'll get you out of any trouble.
> I'll give you the best of care
>   if you'll only get to know and trust me.
> Call me and I'll answer, be at your side in bad times;
>   I'll rescue you, then throw you a party.
> I'll give you a long life,
>   give you a long drink of salvation!'"

If you're dealing with sickness, a relational issue, financial burdens, or discouragement, God is saying to you today, "Let me help you, My beloved." The same God who worked miracles in the Bible will work miracles for you. He parted the sea, raised Lazarus from the dead, sent ravens to feed Elijah, and healed all who came to Him. That same rescuing, loving God is saying to you right now, "I am your good Shepherd. Relax! I got it! I will help you and rescue you."

He Guides Us

Psalm 23:3b, NIV—"He guides me along the right paths for his name's sake."

Psalm 23:3b, TPT—"He opens before me pathways to God's pleasure and leads me along in his footsteps of righteousness so that I can bring honor to his name."

God is a good Shepherd and Father who desires to lead us to good things. Sometimes we wonder what to do next in our lives. God doesn't just lead us to the right places; He also leads us to the right way of living life. It's not always about the "right" location or the "right" decision. He's with us at every step of our journey, and He wants us to tell Him our heart's desires. He asks, "What do you want to do, My child? Where do you want to go? What brings you joy?"

He leads us and guides us into good things, but He doesn't want to control us. He's involved in our lives and knows us uniquely. His desire is to fulfill the longings of our heart that'll bring joy to Him and us. But, in doing so, He sees the whole picture that we don't see, and He guides us accordingly.

God is so good. The revelation that you and I have of His goodness right now is just a glimpse of how good He is. Discovering His goodness could take an eternity. He's so loving that even if we make a wrong decision, He'll cause good to come from it.

He's working out good in your life at this very moment and will help you get back on the right path.

The phrase, "his name's sake," in this verse refers to a shepherd's reputation. If a shepherd lost his flock or left the flock in the wilderness, his reputation would be ruined. God is a good Shepherd who'll never lead you down the wrong path. He'll never lose you or leave you to fend for yourself. God is love, and love doesn't behave like that. God protects His name.

One of the purposes of this book is to share with others how good God is. People often blame God for things He doesn't do or allow. He gets blamed for taking people's lives early or allowing someone to be abused or murdered. But, we all have a free will and can be influenced by the enemy for evil. Jesus came to give us a life of abundance, not evil. People need to know what God is truly like in order to receive His love and all the benefits and promises that He's given us.

He Never Leaves Us

Psalm 23:4a, NIV—"Even though I walk through the darkest valley, I will fear no evil, for you are with me."

Psalm 23:4a, TPT—"Lord, even when your path takes me through the valley of deepest darkness, fear will never conquer me, for you already have! You remain close to me and lead me through it all the way."

In order to find a lush patch of grass where the sheep can graze, shepherds sometimes had to travel through rough terrain and even journey at night. Even so, the sheep trusted that their shepherd would get them where they needed to be and that they were going somewhere good. They kept their eyes on their shepherd and followed his lead.

The sheep had full confidence that the shepherd would never leave them or abandon them. In the same way, we can trust that even when we go through trials, our Father is working out a good outcome for us. We can trust Him with full confidence to lead us and guide us in getting us to the other side when we focus on Him instead of the trials. We're promised in His Word that He'll never leave us no matter what (Hebrews 13:5). God is trustworthy.

God doesn't cause bad things or trials to occur in our lives. They happen as a result of living in a fallen world and because we have a free will to bring bad circumstances upon ourselves. In fact, the Bible promises that trials will be a part of our lives:

> **John 16:33, AMP**—"I have told you these things, so that in Me you may have [perfect] peace. In the world you have tribulation *and* distress *and* suffering, but be courageous [be confident, be undaunted, be filled with joy]; I have overcome the world. [My conquest is accomplished, My victory abiding.]"

However, God is so good and loving that He desires to help us through the difficult patches in our lives and lead us to victory (2 Corinthians 2:14). He's a good Father and is good all the time.

He's unchanging, solid, trustworthy, and loving. He's our rescuing Father who is not moved by our messes. He's not stressed when we wander off the path. He's a God of love and grace who has compassion on us as we go through trials. He cares about what we care about. He tells us, "Child, I want you to learn to trust that I'm good and only have your best interests at heart. I want to help you. I love you. Listen for My voice leading you and helping you in your times of need."

He Protects Us

Psalm 23:4b, NIV—"Your rod and your staff, they comfort me." The Hebrew word for *comfort* in this verse means "to give rest."[8]

Psalm 23:4b, TPT—"Your authority is my strength and my peace. The comfort of your love takes away my fear. I'll never be lonely, for you are near."

Shepherds protected their sheep by using rods and staffs to ward off wild animals. Their staff was bent and could be used to pull sheep that wandered off the path or out of places like holes or tangled bushes where they might get stuck. The staff was a comfort to the sheep, and along with the rod, represented protection and care.

Our loving Father is our protector. He is our helper, and we need His help. We need Him to rescue us at times, and He's more than willing to help us back onto the right path. Our safety and well-being matter to Him.

Sheep have no defense mechanisms. They don't have horns or fangs or claws to defend themselves; therefore, they must rely on their shepherd to defend them. God created sheep to be unable to defend themselves. Likewise, we were also created to not defend ourselves. When we try to attack others, we're not being who God created us to be. He wants to be our defender. He'll either lead us to say something or to remain quiet, but He's our vindicator, so we don't have to—and shouldn't—vindicate ourselves (Romans 12:19).

Verse 5 continues to describe how the Lord deals with our ene-mies—all those things that may come against us in life:

> **Psalm 23:5, NLT**—"You prepare a table before me in the presence of my enemies. You anoint my head with oil; my cup overflows."

> **Psalm 23:5, TPT**—"You become my delicious feast even when my enemies dare to fight. You anoint me with the fragrance of your Holy Spirit; you give me all I can drink of you until my heart overflows."

Sometimes when the sheep grazed in the lush, green pastures, there were snake holes in the soil. The shepherd would pour oil into these holes and also put oil on the sheep's head. The snakes hated the smell of the oil, and it made it difficult for them to come out of the slippery holes. As a result, the sheep were able to graze on the grass safely in the "presence of their enemies." They could eat in confidence, knowing they were being taken care of by a good shepherd. They could feast in peace!

This is a beautiful picture of resting in the finished work of Christ. Jesus took the curse upon Himself at the cross, and we are the blessed recipients of His work. He defeated our enemies of sickness, sin, death, sorrow, depression, shame, and every other thing that doesn't belong to us in Christ. Because He took care of our enemies, we can live in confidence, knowing we're victorious in life. In a world filled with fear of sickness and disease and evil, we're able to live like overcomers.

Just because Jesus defeated our enemies on the cross, however, doesn't mean we no longer have to deal with them. But, we have been promised victory over them. Jesus said in Luke 10:19, "I have given you authority to trample on snakes and scorpions and to overcome all the power of the enemy; nothing will harm you" (NIV). Jesus gave us His authority over all aspects of the enemy, including his lies that come to deceive us. He's given us His truth to counter those lies. But, we have to know what we've been given so we can use it.

God has equipped us with the exact authority that Jesus had while on the earth. That's good news! We have authority to reign in life. When we truly understand that we're righteous, forgiven, and loved children of God, whom the enemy has no power over, it'll cause confidence to rise inside of us. When we know that we know that we know that we have a good Daddy who adores us and thinks the world of us and has already conquered everything that could come against us, it'll cause us to live the abundant life that Jesus came to give us:

John 10:10, MSG—"A thief is only there to steal and kill and destroy. I came so they can have real and eternal life, more and better life than they ever dreamed of."

Aside from protecting the sheep from snakes, shepherds also used oil to rid the sheep of insects that harassed them. If the shepherd didn't get rid of the insects, a sheep would often bang its head against a rock trying to do so, which sometimes led to the sheep's death. Since sheep can't rest if they're being tormented by parasites and bugs, they'll do whatever necessary to be free of them.

Shepherds also used olive oil to prevent infection of a sheep's wounds and cuts. When Jesus was praying in the Garden of Gethsemane before He went to Calvary, He said to His disciples, "My soul is crushed with grief to the point of death" (Mark 14:34, NLT). As mentioned in Chapter 1, *Gethsemane* means "oil press," and olives are crushed to produce oil.

Jesus was "crushed" at the cross. His broken body destroyed sin, death, sickness, and everything that could possibly harm us. He also fulfilled the Law and brought us into a new covenant of grace. We can no longer be accused of wrong doings and sin because sin is gone! First Corinthians 15:56 says the strength of sin is the Law, so if we're no longer bound by the Law, and Jesus removed sin as far as the east is from the west, then no sin can be charged to our account. Because of what Jesus did on the cross, we can now ignore those pestering parasites, or those voices of condemnation, accusation, guilt, and insecurity.

Also, because Jesus was crushed at the cross, healing belongs to us. In the New Testament, anointing oil is used to pray for the sick. James 5:14–15 instructs those who are sick to "¹⁴...call for the elders of the church to come and pray over you, anointing you with oil in the name of the Lord. ¹⁵Such a prayer offered in faith will heal the sick, and the Lord will make you well" (NLT). Jesus already provided our healing; we just receive it in faith. God is a good Father who wants to see us walking in the healing and wholeness that He provided. When He sees us receiving all that He provided, it brings joy to His heart, just like the shepherd who wants to see all of his sheep thriving in his care.

If you're having trouble receiving what God has provided for you, ask Him to help you, and He will. Ask Him to show you any lies you might believe that could hinder you from experiencing His promises. Maybe you don't believe you're qualified to receive from God because you think you've failed too many times. Maybe that voice of accusation tells you that you lack faith. Take it all to Him, and ask Him to show you the truth. As you keep your eyes on your good Shepherd, He'll lead you into the truth.

Jesus has provided us a banquet table of healing, love, joy, restored relationships, prosperity, healing, confidence, peace, and so much more. He enjoys seeing us feasting at this table. All of these blessings come from Him. We're blessed with all spiritual blessings because the life of Christ (all those things listed above) lives in us. Our spirit is perfect because Jesus is perfect.

Psalm 23:5 ends with the phrase, "my cup overflows" (NIV), or, in *The Passion Translation*, "my heart overflows." God is the God of abundance. He is a "more than enough," "over the top," generous God. He provided more than enough wine at the wedding and made enough loaves of bread and fish to feed the 5,000 and still have leftovers! We're filled with His Spirit, and in the overflow of His Spirit giving us everything we need, we can spread the good news wherever we go.

In *Hold On to Hope*, I shared a story of how I told the Father that I wanted to find at least one cardinal feather in my life before I went to heaven because of the special meaning they had to me. Not only did God give me the one feather I asked for, but I've since found twelve others. I've found even more since the publication of *Hold On to Hope*. God loves to give us our heart's desires and even more. He truly is the God of overflow.

He Is Our Future

Psalm 23:6, NIV—"Surely your goodness and love will follow me all the days of my life, and I will dwell in the house of the LORD forever."

Psalm 23:6, TPT—"So why would I fear the future? For your goodness and love pursue me all the days of my life. Then afterward, when my life is through, I'll return to your glorious presence to be forever with you!"

It's important for us to know in our hearts that God is good all the time. He always has good planned for our lives. This doesn't mean we won't go through trials, but when we do, we have the most powerful being in the universe on our side. We have favor. We are loved. We are cherished. And honestly, even when we pass away from this earth, we win! He conquered death for us, and we just pass from here to there.

Isaiah 53:5 tells us that by the stripes of Jesus we have been healed, and this healing is for our present circumstances, whether we have symptoms in our body or not. Yet, whether we are here or there, we still win. When we understand this, it can bring peace to our heart and mind.

Knowing and understanding the relentless love of our good Father toward us is key to receiving from Him. His love is my favorite thing to talk about. When we have confidence that He loves us, always has our best interests at heart, and rescues us as many times as we need rescuing, we'll be safe and secure in our true identity in Christ. Then, fear and anxiety about the future will dissipate. We can then declare as David did, "Why would I fear the future?"

At this very moment, your heavenly Father is working out good in your life and the situations you're facing. He'll never lead you down the wrong path. He knows you intimately and knows your name. You can trust Him with your life. You can trust Him to take care of you. You can trust Him to provide for your every need. And, you can trust Him to never abandon you. He's a good Daddy, who is always consistent and never changing.

Take a moment and pray this to your heavenly Father:

Father, I thank You for the revelation that You're a good Shepherd and good Father. I want to continue to grow in the knowledge of Your love for me and in Your goodness. Thank You for helping me in my everyday life. Thank You for working out my life for good and for rescuing me, even when I get myself into my own mess. Your love for me is amazing and brings me great joy. Thank You for being a good Father. Thank You for choosing me to be Your precious child. Help me to understand more and more just how much You treasure and adore me. In Your precious name I pray. Amen.

CHAPTER 4

THERE IS NOTHING WRONG WITH YOU

One of my mentors asked me a question that sparked the premise for this chapter: How would your life change if you didn't think there was anything wrong with you? I had never thought about that before, and it made me ponder how my life would be different if I could receive the truth (God's truth) about me in my heart. I could believe it in some areas of my life, but in other areas, I didn't fully have the revelation in my heart.

There are many who would consider this question prideful. Yet, for believers, it's true that there's nothing wrong with us. We're comprised of a body, a soul, and a spirit. Our spirit is the part of us that's complete and perfect—whole, spotless, blameless, and righteous—because of Jesus.

Even though we're perfect in Christ, the world continually tries to make us focus on all that is wrong. Proof of this is how there's rarely anything positive mentioned in news reports. The news media today always focus on negativity and what's wrong in the world. There's certainly a time and a place for this, but if we stay focused on the negative all the time, and only see what we deem as negative qualities or behaviors in our own lives, we'll eventually experience negative emotions.

What we dwell on manifests in our feelings. If you grew up in an atmosphere of negativity and criticism, it'll take some time to retrain your brain to break free of these mindsets. Our loving Father is patient and understands your past. He knows why you think the way you do, and He'll help you. So, give yourself grace during your journey of turning your negative thoughts into positive ones.

Aside from the media, often there are people in our lives who are specialists at pointing out every little flaw or weakness they see in us. Relationships can't thrive in an atmosphere of fault finding. When people point out the positive traits instead, calling out your true identity in Christ and not your mistakes, those relationships will flourish.

However, some of us, including myself, fall into the trap of fault finding. I grew up in an atmosphere of negativity and have had to rewire my brain to see things positively. People who are conditioned to trauma oftentimes expect the worst. They get fearful when someone asks, "Can I talk to you about something?" I'm still walking out of some of this myself. It takes a revelation from the Father to start viewing the positive in life instead of what is wrong all the time, but it's so freeing when we do.

The question from my mentor was powerful, considering that my entire childhood was filled with verbal and nonverbal messages telling me that there was something wrong with me. I was raised by parents and step-parents who were wounded themselves and didn't know how to love me in a healthy way.

Changing Our Core Beliefs

When verbal, physical, and sexual abuse is brought on, especially by a parent, it's easy to believe at your core that there's something fundamentally wrong with you. I believed I was unlovable, unwanted, defective, flawed, and that everyone around me agreed with my diagnosis. I always felt that I never measured up in school or in social situations. Even today, it saddens me to see the picture of myself as a little girl swinging on the swing alone at recess. I might as well have worn a sign that read: "Beware! Don't come near me! There's something wrong with me!" That was my foundational belief system. My abusive, defective childhood and the resulting broken mindsets were the main reasons I fell apart later in life and spent years in psych wards, outpatient programs, and visiting psychiatrists.

Psychiatrists are professionals at telling you what's wrong with you. I was used to talking with them about my life, having them ask questions, and watching them document what was wrong with me. A new diagnosis usually meant new or adjusted medications. Writing the "problem" on paper only confirmed to me that there was definitely something "wrong" with me because, after all, they were professionals.

The years I spent in and out of medical offices and psychiatric hospitals only proved to solidify the mindset that I was "defective and abnormal." These doctors, who had studied the mind and had many degrees hanging on their walls, proved on paper that there definitely was "something wrong with me, and it was incurable." They even listed what was wrong: "...bipolar...

PTSD...anxiety disorder...episodes of mania and depression...
suicidal...at risk...." I believed in my heart all that they said and
continued living out my new identities.

For those of you who may be struggling with anything that I
mentioned above, know that God absolutely loves and cherishes
you. He doesn't view you as His bipolar, suicidal, depressed child.
He views you through the eyes of His Spirit. Once you receive
the gift of Jesus and what He's done for you, you're perfect, and
there's nothing wrong with you. This is because Jesus now lives
on the inside of you, and you have His perfect righteousness,
perfect healing, perfect wholeness, perfect love, perfect mind,
perfect joy, and perfect peace.

The Word of God is often the exact opposite of what the world
says. We must know what God says to experience His truth and
freedom. This comes through a process of renewing our mind
and walking in the spirit. Walking in the spirit simply means to
draw on the life and power of the Holy Spirit, who lives in you
as a believer, instead of following the ways of the flesh, or emotions and harmful desires. If our flesh wants to be stressed, for
instance, we can choose instead to walk in the peace that Jesus
has provided for us. The more we know how much we are loved
and accepted by God and who we are in Christ, the more we'll
be drawn to walking in the spirit and the freedom Jesus gave us.

I didn't realize all those years that my identity wasn't based on
my actions. Because of this, my negative mindset that believed
there was something wrong with me was forced deeper into my
heart whenever I failed. When I was born again around the age

of ten, I didn't understand what took place on the inside of me. This is why I continued to receive the negative voices that told me I was something contrary to what the Word of God said, and it was why I received the labels the doctors gave me.

Imagine what the world would be like if we all knew who we are in Christ. And, imagine if we all saw each other for who we are in the spirit and not in the flesh. What a different life we would have! Second Corinthians 5:16 tells us, "Therefore from now on we recognize no one according to the flesh" (NASB). We have the ability to see others as God sees them, but first we must see ourselves the way He sees us. We first must know and experience His love in our own lives before we can pass it on to others.

God wants us to know that we're perfect and beautiful in His sight. He wants us to know that we are loved and accepted. He's a good Father who is relentless in telling us what's right about us.

Jesus Made Everything Right

There was a time when there was a lot wrong with mankind. After the Fall in the Garden of Eden, because of Adam's choice to eat of the forbidden fruit (Genesis 3), we were separated from the Father. But later, God sent Jesus to earth to make everything right: "For God was in Christ, reconciling the world to himself, no longer counting people's sins against them. And he gave us this wonderful message of reconciliation" (2 Corinthians 5:19, NLT). When we receive the gift of salvation by believing in Jesus and what He did for us, all that was wrong with us becomes right because He now lives in us, and we are new creations.

In the Old Testament, mankind lived under God's Law—a system of blessings and curses that are listed in Deuteronomy 28. Man tried to follow all of the Law but kept failing. The Law was good and holy and contained the promise of blessing, but man could never fully adhere to it. The Law couldn't change people's hearts; only Jesus could do this. The Law showed us our need for a Savior.

Jesus fulfilled the Law on our behalf when we couldn't do it ourselves, and because of Jesus, we're blessed and not cursed. He became a curse on the cross (Galatians 3:13) and completely removed everything that was against us. He took our sin upon Himself and gave us His gift of righteousness. He took curses and sickness and left them in the grave. He destroyed the works of the enemy and gave us His authority over sickness, disease, obstacles, and storms. Jesus loved sinners, healed the sick, worked miracles, and spent time with the marginalized and outcast. He came to make everything right. As we receive His gift of salvation and life, we can now say, "I am the righteousness of God in Christ, and there's nothing wrong with me."

One of the greatest reasons that Jesus came to earth was to show us the Father and His heart of love. In fact, in John 14:9, Jesus said, "Anyone who has seen me has seen the Father" (NIV). At the time Jesus arrived on earth, the Jews of Israel didn't know the true heart of the Father. They knew Him as a God of cursing or blessing based on their behavior. Jesus revealed to us that God's heart was never to give us the Law, but it was to have an unbroken relationship with man. Jesus showed us that the Father's heart was always to love and not condemn. He came to "right" His Father's reputation.

Jesus brought us out of the old covenant and into the new, which has better promises. It has promises of healing, deliverance, salvation, life, peace, a God who will never leave us, and so much more. He came to give us a new heart and establish our identity as children of God. He came to show us the true heart of the Father, so we'd know who He really is. I once heard a minister say, "He was the Father's love language on the earth."

How Did Jesus Make Us Right?

Under the old covenant, when people sinned, they were required to bring a sacrifice, such as a lamb, to the priest. First, the priest examined the lamb to ensure it had no blemishes. It had to be flawless to be sacrificed. The Old Testament lamb was a foreshadowing of Jesus, who is called the "Lamb of God," who takes away the sin of the world (John 1:29). Jesus was perfect and sinless.

Once the priest determined that the sacrifice was perfect, the sinner who brought the lamb placed his hands on it, signifying that all of his sin was going into the lamb. In turn, the perfection of the lamb was transferred to the sinner. This symbolized the gift of righteousness Jesus gave to us, as He was the final perfect sacrifice for all time.

Because the lamb now had the sin upon itself, it had to be killed. The person who sinned was made to slit the throat of the animal. Watching the innocent animal shed its blood and die gave the sinner the revelation that his sin caused an innocent animal to die, and because of the animal sacrifice, the sinner could go free.

Families who raised animals for sacrifices would sometimes become attached to them. Being an animal lover myself, I can't imagine going through this. I'm so glad I was born after the cross! Raising animals, paying for them, taking them to the priest, and then killing them was work. People in the Old Testament had to work to have their sins covered. Sins couldn't be fully removed until Jesus became sin for us and removed it at the cross. Jesus worked for us. He went to the cross and to the grave, fulfilling the Law on our behalf. He took all of the consequence and judgment for sin and brought us into a new covenant. We can rejoice that Jesus did it all for us!

When sinners came before the priest with an offering, the priest didn't examine them; he examined their sacrifice. In the same way, when God views the final sacrifice of Jesus on the cross, and we receive what He did by faith, He says, "My child, there's nothing wrong with you! You are righteous. My Son made you righteous." Because of what Jesus did for us, we can boldly declare, "There's nothing wrong with me!"

I don't believe it was ever God's heart to give the Law to mankind. Yet, when people broke the Law, the sacrifices brought grace and forgiveness into their situation. God knew that hearts couldn't truly be changed until Jesus came to dwell in us, but this system of sacrifices helped people move forward after a failure. The sacrifices' blood couldn't remove guilt and shame, but the blood of Jesus can. The animal sacrifices were simply a shadow of things to come, pointing to the real thing—Jesus.

Now that we have Jesus, and He perfected us with His one-time sacrifice, we don't need to live with sin-consciousness anymore.

He doesn't want us living with guilt and shame, which only increases the cycle of sin. He wants us to know that He sees us as perfect and blameless, so we never run from Him, especially when we fail.

We may try to run, but we'll never be separated from Him because we're forever one with Him. He wants us to have a real relationship with Him without fear of punishment. He may correct us with His Word, but He doesn't punish us by causing bad things to happen or putting sickness on us, as many believe. He's a good Father who only wants the best for His children, including you!

Truths from the Word

The following scriptures will help bring revelation concerning what Jesus' sacrifice at the cross did for us and what we now have in Him:

Hebrews 10:1–18, TPT—
Christ's Eternal Sacrifice

"¹The old system of living under the law presented us with only a faint shadow, a crude outline of the reality of the wonderful blessings to come. Even with its steady stream of sacrifices offered year after year, there still was nothing that could make our hearts perfect before God. ²⁻³For if animal sacrifices could once and for all eliminate sin, they would have ceased to be offered and the worshipers would have clean consciences. Instead, once was not enough so by the repetitive sacrifices year after year, the worshipers were continually reminded of their sins, with their hearts still impure. ⁴For what power does the blood of bulls and goats have to remove sin's guilt? ⁵So when Jesus the Messiah came into the world he said, 'Since your ultimate desire was not another animal sacrifice,

you have clothed me with a body
that I might offer myself instead!
⁶Multiple burnt offerings and sin-offerings
cannot satisfy your justice.
⁷So I said to you, "God—
I will be the One to go and do your will,
to fulfill all that is written of me in your Word!"'

⁸First he said, 'Multiple burnt-offerings and sin-offerings cannot satisfy your justice' (even though the law required them to be offered). ⁹And then he said, 'God, I will be the One to go and do your will.' *So by being the sacrifice that removes sin*, he abolishes animal sacrifices and replaces that entire system with the new covenant. ¹⁰By God's will we have been purified and made holy once and for all through the sacrifice of the body of Jesus, the Messiah!

¹¹Yet every day priests still serve, ritually offering the same sacrifices again and again—sacrifices that can never take away sin's guilt. ¹²But when this Priest had offered the one supreme sacrifice for sin for all time he sat down on a throne at the right hand of God, ¹³waiting until all his whispering enemies are subdued and turn into his footstool. ¹⁴And by his one perfect sacrifice he made us perfectly holy and complete for all time!

¹⁵The Holy Spirit confirms this to us by this Scripture, for the Lord says,

¹⁶'Afterwards, I will give them this covenant: I will embed my laws into their hearts and fasten my Word to their thoughts.'

¹⁷And then he says,

'I will not ever again remember their sins and lawless deeds!'

¹⁸So if our sins have been forgiven and forgotten, why would we ever need to offer another sacrifice for sin?"

Notice that verse 14 says, "…by his one perfect sacrifice he made us perfectly holy and complete for all time!" Because of Jesus, we can say, "There is nothing wrong with me!" Again, this is referring to our position of identity, not behavior. We will continue to mess up. I just did last night! I had to remind myself, "I'm a righteous girl!" But now when the voice of accusation comes to point out everything wrong about you (things you still struggle with), just remember everything that's right about you. Jesus took all our past, present, and future sins! That's great news!

2 Corinthians 5:21, AMP—"He made Christ who knew no sin to [judicially] be sin on our behalf, so that in Him we would become the righteousness of God [that is, we would be made acceptable to Him and placed in a right relationship with Him by His gracious lovingkindness]."

Colossians 1:21–22, TPT—"Even though you were once distant from him, living in the shadows of your evil thoughts and actions, he reconnected you back to himself. *He released his supernatural peace to you* through the sacrifice of his own body as the sin-payment on your behalf so that you would dwell in his presence. And now there is nothing between you and Father God, for he sees you as **holy, flawless, and restored**." (emphasis mine)

It's only because of the blood that Jesus shed for us that we can have a clean conscious and be declared innocent. It's only because of Jesus that we don't have to live with a sin-consciousness but can have a righteousness-consciousness, which brings rest, joy, and peace. It's only because of Jesus that we can now say, "There's nothing wrong with me!"

Jesus could've just had His throat slit like the animal sacrifices of the Old Testament, and that would've been enough to take care of the sin of the entire world. Instead, Jesus was also willingly beaten, broken, ripped to shreds, humiliated, and mocked, I believe, to show us that He also paid the price for sickness, guilt, shame, and everything else that was against us. We are now blessed with every spiritual blessing because of Jesus (Ephesians 1:3). It's all Him! We just simply receive and say, "Thank You."

He earned this for us. We don't have to earn His love or acceptance. He wants us to rest in His perfect opinion of us and have a relationship without us fearing His anger or punishment. He wants us to know that we're fully accepted and that He views us as flawless.

Ephesians 1:3, TPT—"Every spiritual blessing in the

heavenly realm has already been lavished upon us as a love gift from our wonderful heavenly Father, the Father of our Lord Jesus—all because he sees us wrapped into Christ. This is why we celebrate him with all our hearts!"

Grace teacher Dr. Paul Ellis, writes: "In the Bible, the word *forgive* literally means to send away. Your sin hasn't merely been overlooked, it has been abolished (AMP), put away (ASV), and removed (GNV). Neither has God put away your sins in the same way that you might put your rubbish in a bin by the back door—close by and smelly. He has removed them from you as far as the east is from the west (Psalm 103:12). If you were to go looking for your sins, you wouldn't find them. They're gone! They've all been blotted out (Isaiah 44:22)."[1]

> **Isaiah 44:22, KJV**—"I have blotted out, as a thick cloud, thy transgressions, and, as a cloud, thy sins: return unto me; for I have redeemed thee."

Our good, loving, heavenly Father wants us to know that we're free from sin, guilt, shame, and that nagging feeling that something is wrong with us. When any voice tells us otherwise, we must retrain our brains to reject those thoughts and meditate on the truth of who we are in Christ. It takes time, but give yourself grace in the process. You'll get there. God will help you as you depend on Him.

> **Hebrews 9:14, TPT**—"Yet how much more will the sacred blood of the Messiah thoroughly cleanse our consciences!"

Cleanse here means "to make clean."[2] Some synonyms of *cleanse* are *disinfect, purge, sanitize, absolve* and *purify.*[3]

The blood of Jesus made clean, disinfected, purged, sanitized, and absolved our consciences from all guilt and shame and not feeling good enough. It's only His precious blood that was shed for us out of pure love that could do that. It brings Him much joy when we receive this truth in our hearts, rest in His truth, and experience the healing and wholeness He provided.

If you're not there yet, don't entertain any voice of accusation now. I know how sly that voice is to try to condemn. Understand that the Father wants you well more that you want it for yourself. His relentless, rescuing, and restoring love will chase you down until you "get it." His love will pursue you until you can truly say and believe, "All is well! There's nothing wrong with me."

> **Romans 5:1, TPT**—"Our faith in Jesus transfers God's righteousness to us and he now declares us flawless in his eyes. This means we can now enjoy true and lasting peace with God, all because of what our Lord Jesus, the Anointed One, has done for us."

Jesus came to make us flawless. The word *flaw* means "a feature that mars the perfection of something; defect; fault."[4] Synonyms of *flaw* are *defect, blemish, deficiency, weakness,* and *weak spot.*[5]

And, *defect* means "a lack of something necessary for completeness or perfection; shortcoming; deficiency."[6]

Romans 5:1 with this expanded definition reads: "Our faith in

Jesus transfers God's righteousness to us and he now declares us without defect, fault, or anything else that mars our perfection; blemish, deficiency, weakness, or weak spot."

Colossians 2:10, AMP—"And in Him you have been made complete..."

Jesus came to make us complete and whole. He came to make everything right that was wrong. The definition of *complete* is "having all parts or elements, lacking nothing, whole, entire; full."[7] Its synonyms are *all, entire, exhaustive, faultless, full, intact, lock stock and barrel, unbroken, uncut, replete, unimpaired, undiminished, whole, the whole enchilada,* and *whole nine yards.*[8]

Inserting the definition of *complete* and its synonyms, Colossians 2:10 reads: "And in Him you have been made complete, having all parts, lacking nothing, whole, entire, full, faultless, unbroken, replete, undiminished, the whole enchilada, whole nine yards."

We Are Complete in Jesus

Jesus is the one who makes us complete. When we understand that true completeness is only found in Him, then we'll stop looking for other things to make us whole. Our human mind, especially for those who've experienced a lot of trauma, wants to take us down the path of negativity. Our mind sometimes wants to show us what we're lacking instead of what we have. According to historians, Adam and Eve had hundreds of trees to eat from, yet the enemy had them focus on the one tree that was off-limits. The same thing can easily happen to us if we're not careful.

I recently experienced abandonment in a relationship. We weren't created for rejection, and my mind temporarily focused on this one relationship that walked away instead of the many relationships that were still in my life. Shifting my mindset to what I still had, instead of focusing on the loss, caused healing to take place. Likewise, focusing on what we don't have instead of what we do have leads to a lack of peace and frustration.

When we realize that in Christ, we have absolutely everything we need with no lack, any earthly losses won't take away our wholeness and completeness in Him. Meditating on this truth results in peace and joy, even during trials. I encourage you to say aloud, "I am complete. Jesus made me whole and complete. I don't need anything else to complete myself. He did it all. Thank You, Jesus!"

Knowing this truth will bring a greater intimacy with Jesus and will affect every relationship around us. When we're able to view ourselves the way He sees us, we can view others in the same way. Then, we can react in love and forgiveness when a wrong is done to us. How we see ourselves affects every area of our lives.

To close this chapter, take a moment and declare the following statements aloud:

I am loved.

I am flawless.

I am accepted.

I am forgiven.

I am righteous.

I will focus on what is right with me in Jesus.

There's nothing wrong with me.

CHAPTER 5

WE WIN!

My friend Christy and I both had boys that played on the same football team. For one of their playoff games, we each had commitments that we couldn't cancel and had to miss the game. But, we knew that the game was being filmed and that we were receiving a copy of the video, so we planned on getting together the following evening to watch it.

My commitment changed, however, and I was able to make it to the game after all, but I never told Christy. After watching the game, I knew, of course, that our team had won, but I didn't want Christy to feel bad about not going, so I pretended that I didn't know what happened.

The next day, Christy came to my house to watch the game with me. I wasn't acting like myself, and I didn't share in her excitement of big plays. When the other team scored, Christy was disappointed and raised her voice at the TV, but I just sat there as calm as can be. She asked me why I was so calm, and I came up with an excuse, hoping she wouldn't learn the truth.

As the game went on, there were scores by both teams, fumbles by both teams, and a lot of exciting plays. As the score went back and forth, Christy's emotions went back and forth. I continued to stay perfectly peaceful. She finally asked me, "What's wrong with you? Why aren't you into this game more?" I couldn't hold it in any longer and finally confessed the truth to her. I yelled out, "Christy, I went to the game yesterday. I already know that we won!" We both screamed excitedly and hugged.

This is a fictitious story, but it illustrates a great point about Christianity. We can relax and rest no matter what comes our way because we know the outcome of our lives: We win! When Jesus gave up His spirit on the cross and declared, "It is finished!" He meant just that—it is finished. He destroyed sin, sickness, anxiety, any diagnosis that's ever been spoken over us, the works of the devil, and more. He conquered death once and for all, and now, even when we pass from this life to heaven, we win!

We're no longer fighting *for* victory, but we're fighting *from* a position of victory. Our fight is only to enforce the enemy's defeat. All we need to do is stand against any opposition that tries to steal the ball (God's provision) from us. That ball can represent healing, peace, finances, relationships, or anything else God has promised us.

If symptoms of sickness hit your body, you can relax knowing that you're already healed and Jesus took care of it. You're on the winning team! You can rest in Him, and He'll show you what to do or not do. He may show you a natural remedy, He may tell you to use your authority or laugh at the devil, or He may lead you to a doctor to help you. I believe God can use many ways to bring us into healing and wholeness. There are some things, though, that doctors can only try to manage. They may tell you that the sickness you have is incurable, or there's nothing else they can do for you. This is when you need to know that you're on the winning team and you've already won.

For years, I didn't know what Jesus did for me. I didn't realize I was already on the winning team. I didn't understand that I was striving to earn what Jesus already provided for me and didn't know "I already had it." I considered myself a bipolar, alcoholic, mentally ill, and defective Christian for years, never believing my behavior would measure up enough for God to heal me. When you hear that bipolar disorder is incurable and you'll never have a sound mind, it makes you believe that you're not on the winning team. When I was told, "You'll always be up and down, and all we can do is hope to manage your disorder effectively with medication," you believe that you're not on the winning team.

In my book *Hold On to Hope*, I share how I ended up switching identities from Team Incurable to Jesus' winning team. I took hold of my healing, and I haven't let go since. It was easy for me to switch my mindset to being on the winning team when it came to bipolar disorder, but in other areas, I needed that daily reminder to stand against lies and opposition with the truth. When I teach, I discuss those things that I need to be reminded of over and over again. Throughout the remainder of this chapter, we'll look at several scriptures to help remind us that we're on the winning team.

We Win Because Our Sins Are Forgiven

Isaiah 43:25, MSG—"But I, yes I, am the one who takes care of your sins—that's what I do. **I don't keep a list of your sins.**" (emphasis mine)

Colossians 2:10–15, TPT—
"¹⁰And **our own completeness is now found in him**. We are completely filled *with God* as Christ's fullness over-flows within us. He is the Head of every kingdom and authority in the universe!
¹¹Through our union with him we have experienced cir-cumcision of heart. **All of the guilt and power of sin has been cut away and is now extinct** because of what Christ, the Anointed One, has accomplished for us.
¹²For we've been buried with him into his death. Our 'baptism into death' also means we were raised with him when we believed in God's resurrection power, the power that raised him from death's realm.
¹³This 'realm of death' describes our former state, for we were held in sin's grasp. But now, we've been resur-rected out of that 'realm of death' never to return, **for we are forever alive and forgiven of all our sins!**
¹⁴**He canceled out every legal violation we had on our record** and the old arrest warrant that stood to indict us. He erased it all—our sins, our stained soul—he deleted it all *and they cannot be retrieved!* Everything we once were in Adam has been placed onto his cross and nailed per-manently there as a public display of cancellation.
¹⁵Then Jesus made a public spectacle of all the powers

and principalities of darkness, stripping away from them every weapon and all their spiritual authority and power to accuse us. And by the power of the cross, Jesus led them around as prisoners in a **procession of triumph**. *He was not their prisoner; they were his!*"
(emphasis mine)

Colossians 2:13–14, AMP—
"¹³When you were dead in your sins and in the uncircumcision of your flesh (worldliness, manner of life), God made you alive together with Christ, having [freely] forgiven us all our sins, ¹⁴having **canceled out** the certificate of debt consisting of legal demands [which were in force] against us and which were hostile to us...."
(emphasis mine)

In the *New American Standard Bible,* the Greek word for *having canceled out* is *exaleipho* (from *ek* and *aleipho*), which literally means "to wipe out, erase, obliterate."[1] Author and Bible commentator Wendell Kent explains that *exaleipho* means "to remove by wiping off, as when a blackboard is erased. The word was applied to the process of obliterating writing on any material. ...The idea in all the uses is to cause something to cease by obliterating or eliminating any evidence."[2]

The definition of *obliterate* is "destroy completely, to wipe out."[3] Some synonyms of *obliterate* are *annihilate, eliminate, decimate, wipe off the face of the earth, wipe off the map, to cause to become invisible, remove all traces of, abolish, do away with,* and *put an end to.*[4]

Putting these definitions together, Colossians 2:13–14 becomes: "¹³...God made you alive together with Christ, having [freely] forgiven us all our sins, [14]having annihilated, eliminated, decimated, wiped off the face of the earth and the map, caused to become invisible, removed all traces of, abolished, done away with, and put an end to the certificate of debt consisting of legal demands [which were in force] against us and which were hostile to us...."

One Bible commentary offers the following explanation of *exaleipho*: "To understand the word *exaleipho* is to understand the amazing mercy and lovingkindness of God. The substance on which ancient documents were written was either papyrus, a kind of paper..., or vellum, a substance made of the skins of animals. Both were fairly expensive and certainly could not be wasted. Ancient ink had no acid in it; it lay on the surface of the paper and did not, as modern ink usually does, bite into it. Sometimes a scribe, to save paper, used papyrus or vellum that had already been written upon. When he did that, he took a sponge and wiped off the writing. Because it was only on the surface of the paper, the ink could be wiped out as if it had never been! God, in his amazing mercy, banished the record of our sins so completely that it was as if it had never been; not a trace remained!"[5]

Not only are we on the winning team, but we have no record of our losses! Our good Father has obliterated all our sin and the record of our sin with the precious blood of Christ.

We Win Because of Grace

Matthew 11:28–30, MSG—"Are you tired? Worn out? Burned out on religion? Come to me. Get away with me and you'll recover your life. I'll show you how to take a real rest. Walk with me and work with me—watch how I do it. Learn the unforced rhythms of grace. I won't lay anything heavy or ill-fitting on you. Keep company with me and you'll learn to live freely and lightly."

If you're tired or worn out, Jesus wants to show you that He set you free from the Law. If you're experiencing anger, bitterness, resentment, depression, or exhaustion, you probably need a reminder that you don't have to earn God's love. You can rest in the finished work of Jesus, in His arms of love and grace.

Romans 5:13, NIV—"To be sure, sin was in the world before the law was given, but sin is not charged against anyone's account where there is no law."

Romans 6:14, TPT—"Remember this: sin will not conquer you, for God already has! You are not governed by law but governed by the reign of the grace of God."

Galatians 5:1, TPT—"Let me be clear, the Anointed One has set us free—not partially, but completely and wonderfully free! We must always cherish this truth and stubbornly refuse to go back into the bondage of our past."

We are "completely and wonderfully" free because of Jesus! We're on the winning team. But, we must be careful that our mind doesn't take us back to being on the wrong team. We must stubbornly refuse to go back to any negative mindsets that take us away from the winning team mentality or thinking we have to do something to earn being on that winning team.

Galatians 5:1 tells us that Jesus is the one who set us free. Paul continued in Galatians 5 to remind the Galatians not to go back to the bondage of the Law. He was trying to tell them that Jesus set them free, so they shouldn't go back to the bondage of circumcision and Jewish regulations to try to make themselves right with God.

We can't earn what Jesus has freely given us. Team Jesus has made us holy, blameless, forgiven, healed, and completely and wonderfully free. And, He's given us eternal life. Our only job is to rest in that by receiving it and thanking Him for it. Even when we're enforcing sickness's defeat in our body, it's from a place of rest and victory.

Again, Colossians 2:13–14 tells us, "¹³...God made you alive together with Christ, having [freely] forgiven us all our sins, ¹⁴having canceled out the **certificate of debt consisting of legal demands** [which were in force] against us and which were hostile to us. And this certificate He has set aside *and* completely removed by nailing it to the cross" (AMP, emphasis mine).

Jesus completely obliterated and wiped out our certificate of decrees against us, which was the system of the Law and the system of earning God's blessings. In the Old Testament, when someone paid off a debt, *tetelestai* was written on the debt certificate, meaning that the debt was paid in full. This is the same word that Jesus used in John 19:30 when He said, "It is finished!"[6] just before He gave up His spirit on the cross. Jesus paid all our debt in full. The old covenant became obsolete by Jesus' blood that was shed in the new covenant.

Jesus set us free from the Law. We're now on Team Jesus, not Team Law! The Law was good, but everyone who tried to keep it failed. Jesus kept the Law and fulfilled it, then moved it out of the way and brought us into the freedom of grace. But, even when we fail and revert back to the Law, we're still winners. And, we know our failures are never recorded because God doesn't keep track of them. When we know that we're forgiven, we don't want to sin and hurt people. God's grace gives us a license to win, not a license to sin!

Love is the fruit of knowing we're on the winning team:

> **John 3:16–17, MSG**—"This is how much God loved the world: He gave His Son, his one and only Son. And this is why: so that **no one need be destroyed;** by believing in him, **anyone can have a whole and lasting life.** God didn't go to all the trouble of sending his Son merely to point an accusing finger, telling the world how bad it was. **He came to help,** to put **the world right again.** Anyone who trusts in him is acquitted...." (emphasis mine)

The following is a comparison of Team Law versus Team Grace.[7]

Law:

- Prohibits (Exodus 20:7–17; Galatians 3:10)
- Condemns (Romans 7:9)
- Says, "Do" (Exodus 20:7–17)
- Curses (Galatians 3:10)
- Slays sinners (Romans 8:2)
- Says, "Continue to be holy" (1 Peter 1:15–16)
- Condemns the best man (James 2:10)
- Says, "Pay what you owe" (Matthew 18:34)
- Says, "Wages of sin is death" (Romans 6:23)
- Reveals sin (Romans 7:7)
- Given by Moses (John 1:17)
- Demands obedience (Exodus 20:7–17; Romans 6:11–13)
- Done away in Christ (2 Corinthians 3:14)
- Shuts every mouth before God (Romans 3:19)
- Written on stone (Exodus 24:12; 31:18)
- Puts us under bondage (Romans 8:15; Galatians 2:4; 5:1)
- Gives knowledge of sin (Romans 3:20)
- Says, "The soul that sinneth, it shall die" (Ezekiel 18:20)
- Death (Romans 8:2)

Grace:

- Invites and gives (Matthew 11:28)
- Redeems (Romans 8:1)
- Says, "It is done" (John 17:4)
- Blesses (Galatians 3:14)
- Makes sinners alive (Romans 8:2)
- Says, "It is finished" (John 19:30)
- Saves the worst man (1 Timothy 1:15)
- Says, "I freely forgive all" (Romans 3:24)
- "The gift of God is eternal life" (Romans 6:23)
- Reconciles sin (2 Corinthians 5:19)

- Came by Jesus Christ (John 1:17)
- Bestows and gives power to obey (Romans 6:11–13)
- Abides forever (John 6:47)
- Opens the mouth to praise God (Psalm 100:4; Colossians 3:16)
- Written in the tablets of the heart (2 Corinthians 3:3)
- Sets us free in liberty of the sons of God (Romans 8:2; Galatians 5:1)
- Gives redemption from sin (Titus 2:11)
- Believe and they shall live (John 2:16)
- Life (Romans 8:2)

Because we're no longer under the Law, we're dead to it and have been delivered from it. We're now under grace and are on the winning team. Jesus is the end of the Law to those who believe (Romans 10:4). Jesus is the one who provided everything on the grace list above. The cross changed everything. Jesus changed everything for us by emptying Himself, coming to earth as a man, disarming our enemy, dying a brutal death, completely forgiving our sins, healing every sickness, and giving us eternal life (His life). His rescuing, relentless, restoring love has set us free!

We Win Because Our Enemy Is Defeated

Colossians 2:15, AMP—"When He had disarmed the rulers and authorities [those supernatural forces of evil operating against us], **He made a public example of them** [exhibiting them as captives in His triumphal procession], having triumphed over them through the cross." (emphasis mine)

During the Roman Empire, whenever a general was victorious in battle, he'd parade his armies through the streets of Rome, with his captives and the valuables they captured following behind. The defeated general would be behind the victorious general, following in a chariot, with a slave holding a jeweled crown over his head to mock him. Behind that general were his defeated armies.

In Colossians 2:15, Paul uses the imagery of this parade to depict Jesus triumphing over our enemies of sickness, poverty, guilt, shame, depression, and so forth. They're defeated forever for everyone to see! In Jesus' death, burial, and resurrection, He won the victory over any enemy we would ever face.

> **2 Corinthians 2:14, AMP**—"But thanks be to God, who always leads us in triumph in Christ, and through us spreads *and* makes evident everywhere the sweet fragrance of the knowledge of Him."

During these victory parades, incense was burned to signify triumph. As God leads us in victory, we exude the sweet fragrance of Jesus. Jesus causes us to be victorious overcomers, and we have the fragrance of an overcomer everywhere we go! Declare right now, "I'm a winner! Others detect the fragrance of Jesus all over me wherever I go."

I encourage you to close your eyes and visualize yourself having a victory parade on your street. Imagine yourself with Jesus in the victory chariot, cheering and celebrating. Now, picture anything you're struggling with behind you in the defeated chariot. You're in the front of the parade with Jesus, while sickness, negative mindsets, relational issues, condemnation, addiction, sin, or any other struggle you have is behind you. All sin and death is behind you. Jesus defeated it all and made you a victorious overcomer.

Jesus has already won the battle for us, so if we're fighting symptoms of sickness or anything else, we're fighting *from* a position of victory, and we're not fighting *for* victory. There's a huge difference. When you know that you already have the victory, it changes everything and brings you into a place of peace and rest. God says, "Relax! I took care of it. Receive it. I will help you."

The forces of darkness have been defeated, but they still exist and will try to steal from you, kill you, and destroy you (John 10:10). God's Word tells us that, although we already have the victory in Jesus, we must be watchful and resist the enemy so he'll flee from us. We must tell him, "No!" A thief can only steal what we already possess. We have to resist and stand against him with the Word.

> **1 Peter 5:8, TPT**—"Be well balanced and always alert, because your enemy, the devil, roams around incessantly, like a roaring lion looking for its prey to devour."

Even though Jesus defeated the enemy, he still tries to "devour" Christians and get us to rejoin his losing team. But, because Jesus stripped him of all power, the only thing he can do is to try to get us to believe his lies. My friend and Bible teacher, Carlie Terradez, says, "Take yourself off the menu," referring to the enemy seeking out prey to devour.

James 4:7, AMP—"So submit to [the authority of] God. Resist the devil [stand firm against him] and he will flee from you."

Matthew 4:1–11, AMPC—

"¹Then Jesus was led (guided) by the [Holy] Spirit into the wilderness (desert) to be tempted (tested and tried) by the devil.

²And He went without food for forty days and forty nights, and later He was hungry.

³And the tempter came and said to Him, If You are God's Son, command these stones to be made [loaves of] bread.

⁴But He replied, **It has been written, Man shall not live *and* be upheld *and* sustained by bread alone, but by every word that comes forth from the mouth of God.**

⁵Then the devil took Him into the holy city and placed Him on a turret (pinnacle, gable) of the temple sanctuary.

⁶And he said to Him, If You are the Son of God, throw Yourself down; for it is written, He will give His angels charge over you, and they will bear you up on their hands, lest you strike your foot against a stone.

⁷Jesus said to him, On the other hand, **it is written also,** You shall not tempt, test thoroughly, *or* try exceedingly the Lord your God.

⁸Again, the devil took Him up on a very high mountain and showed Him all the kingdoms of the world and the glory (the splendor, magnificence, preeminence, and excellence) of them.

⁹And he said to Him, These things, all taken together, I

will give You, if You will prostrate Yourself before me and do homage *and* worship me.

¹⁰Then Jesus said to him, Begone, Satan! For it has been written, You shall worship the Lord your God, and Him alone shall you serve.

¹¹Then the devil departed from Him, and behold, angels came and ministered to Him."

(emphasis mine)

When it comes to resisting the enemy, there are many ways to do so, but it all comes back to knowing who we are in Christ and the authority we have. God may lead you to meditate on the fact that Jesus has made you an overcomer and ignore what the devil is trying to throw at you. Or, He may instruct you to laugh at him. The devil doesn't like anything that has to do with joy. God may have you speak to your mountain of trouble and command it to leave in Jesus' name. Or, you may just need to say, "Help me, Jesus!" He'll come to your rescue and give you His strength to know what to do or not do. God will also lead you in rest. You can resist in a place of rest.

Knowledge of His love, grace, victory, and who we are in Christ and what He says about us will bring us into an overcoming life. We may get tempted to be stressed, worried, and fearful, which are all part of the enemy's team, but we just need to remember that we already have the victory in Christ.

If you find yourself anxious or worried, or if you're struggling with sin or negative mindsets, know that Jesus will help you get to the other side of victory because victory belongs to you. You won't always make the journey to victory perfectly, and the Father doesn't expect perfection from you. That's why we needed a Savior to rescue us. The only one who lived perfectly is Jesus.

If you fail, get back up, dust your feet off, and continue to move forward. You can do it! The Father believes in you and has faith in you. He's waiting to help you and share His wisdom and strategies with you. He wants nothing more than to see you walking in the victory that Jesus paid for you to have.

When we're able to see ourselves as victorious, we're also able to freely give away what Jesus has given us. When we know who we are in Him, we can change the world because we have His victorious life, and we'll allow His life to break out of us into the people and situations around us. I love to see people healed and set free. There's nothing I enjoy more than making Jesus famous.

In addition, when we see ourselves as overcomers, we won't allow failures to keep us in condemnation. We know we're righteous, so we can continue to resist that voice of accusation with our heads held high. Victorious overcomers never look down in shame because we know that shame doesn't belong to us. If you still struggle with sin or failure, and you have a hard time letting it go and seeing yourself as an overcomer, now is your moment to receive the victory that Jesus paid for. Picture that struggle or sin nailed to the cross as if it never existed, because that's exactly how God sees it.

Colossians 2:14, PHILLIPS—"Christ has utterly wiped out the damning evidence of broken laws and commandments which always hung over our heads, and has completely annulled it by nailing it over his own head on the cross."

That's good news! Jesus put us on the winning team!

CHAPTER 6

FORGET NOT ALL HIS BENEFITS

Consider the following scenario:

Jody, an American businesswoman, goes on a business trip for a week in France. Not only is this a country that she has always dreamed of visiting, but she gets to go for free. After Jody arrives in France and settles into her hotel, she has the whole day to visit and explore. She's walking the streets of Paris when suddenly a man, noticing that she's dressed like a tourist, offers her a free ticket for a bus tour of Paris that he can't use. She excitedly accepts the ticket and thanks the man.

Later that day, Jody boards the tour bus with other tourists and learns that the first stop is the Eiffel Tower. When they arrive, everyone gets off the bus, except for Jody. All those who got off enjoyed seeing the Eiffel Tower in person and received free pictures that were taken of them at the tower as part of the bus tour ticket they purchased. While they were gone, Jody sat in the bus, gazing out the window.

The next stop is the world famous Louvre Art Museum. The bus tour includes a free ticket to the museum, along with a photo taken next to the "Mona Lisa." When the bus stops, everyone again gets off except for Jody, who continues to look out the window. After the Louvre, the bus stops at Notre Dame, the famous Parisian church built in 1163. Aside from a tour of the church, this stop includes free French crepes! Again, everyone departs the bus except for Jody.

After all the tourists returned to the bus, the bus driver dropped everyone off where the tour began. As people were leaving, one man asked Jody, "Why did you just stay on the bus the whole time?" Jody replied, "I thought my ticket just included the bus ride. I didn't realize that all the other benefits were for me to enjoy as well."

I know this story sounds too ridiculous to actually be true, but it's a picture of many in the body of Christ who don't realize all the benefits that Christ has given them. When we don't know our benefits, it's as if we never had them. Or, if we forget the benefits we have, we won't be able to enjoy everything the Father has for us in this life. God wants us to get off the bus and experience all of His blessings.

Our Benefits Package

God wants to see us succeeding and walking in all of His promises, which are "Yes" and "Amen!" in Christ (2 Corinthians 1:20). It brings Him great joy when we know what belongs to us. This is why we need to keep hearing the gospel over and over again. Romans 10:17 says, "…faith comes by hearing, and hearing by the word of God" (NKJV). Many Bible translations read: "…faith comes by hearing the word of Christ." Faith comes by hearing what Christ did for us! We need to meditate on the finished work of Christ every day so we can know with certainty who we are and what we have in Him.

Psalm 103 is a great place to see some of the amazing benefits God wants us to remember:

> "¹Praise the LORD, my soul;
>   all my inmost being, praise his holy name.
> ²Praise the LORD, my soul,
>   and **forget not** all his benefits —
> ³who forgives all your sins
>   and heals all your diseases,
> ⁴who redeems your life from the pit
>   and crowns you with love and compassion,
> ⁵who satisfies your desires with good things
>   so that your youth is renewed like the eagle's.
> ⁶The LORD works righteousness
>   and justice for all the oppressed.
> ¹⁰he does not treat us as our sins deserve
>   or repay us according to our iniquities.
> ¹¹For as high as the heavens are above the earth,
>   so great is his love for those who fear him;
> ¹²as far as the east is from the west,
>   so far has he removed our transgressions from us."
> (vv. 1–6, 10–12, NIV, emphasis mine)

The Message Bible translates verses 1–6 this way:

> "¹⁻²O my soul, bless GOD.
>   From head to toe, I'll bless his holy name!
> O my soul, bless GOD,
>   **don't forget** a single blessing!
> ³⁻⁵He forgives your sins—every one.

He heals your diseases—every one.

He redeems you from hell—saves your life!

He crowns you with love and mercy—a paradise crown.

He wraps you in goodness—beauty eternal.

He renews your youth—you're always young in his presence.

⁶GOD makes everything come out right;

he puts victims back on their feet."

(emphasis mine)

And, *The Passion Translation* reads:

"¹With my whole heart, with my whole life,

and with my innermost being,

I bow in wonder and love before you, the holy God!

²Yahweh, you are my soul's celebration.

How could I ever forget the miracles of kindness

you've done for me?

³You kissed my heart with forgiveness, in spite of all I've done.

You've healed me inside and out from every disease.

⁴You've rescued me from hell and saved my life.

You've crowned me with love and mercy.

⁵You satisfy my every desire with good things.

You've supercharged my life so that I soar again

like a flying eagle in the sky!

⁶You're a God who makes things right,

giving justice to the defenseless.

⁷You unveiled to Moses your plans

and showed Israel's sons what you could do.
⁸Lord, you're so kind and tenderhearted
to those who don't deserve it
and so patient with people who fail you!
Your love is like a flooding river
overflowing its banks with kindness."
(vv. 1–8, emphasis mine)

From these verses, it's obvious there are some things the Father does not want us to forget, including that...

- He's forgiven us, no matter what we've done
- He's already healed us of every disease
- He's rescued us and saved us
- He's crowned us with love and mercy
- He's satisfied our every desire with good things
- He makes us soar again
- He makes things right because He's our defender, and He works good from both good and bad situations
- He's kind and tenderhearted toward us, and He's faithful when we're not
- He's patient with us, especially when we fail; He has no condemnation
- His love is like a flooding river; we're flooded with His love!

Our benefits package is absolutely amazing, and it's a love gift to us from our good, heavenly Father.

We Need Help Remembering

Even though we see the words, "don't forget" in Psalm 103, we do still forget. But, remember, there's no condemnation when we do. God knew we'd forget from time to time, which is another reason He gave us His written Word.

Consider the Israelites. God performed amazing miracles for the children of Israel while freeing them from the bondage of slavery in Egypt. In Exodus 14:21–31, we read where Moses "…stretched out his hand over the sea, and all that night the LORD drove the sea back with a strong east wind and turned it into dry land…" (NIV). God divided the waters, and the Egyptians drown chasing after the Israelites, who then miraculously walked through the sea on dry land, arriving safely on the other side.

Can you imagine seeing the Red Sea being divided before your eyes? You'd think after witnessing this miracle firsthand, they'd never forget what God did for them, but over time, they forgot this miracle along with many others God performed on their behalf.

"¹¹**They forgot** what he had done,
   the wonders he had shown them.
¹²He did miracles in the sight of their ancestors
   in the land of Egypt, in the region of Zoan.
¹³He divided the sea and led them through;
   he made the water stand up like a wall.
¹⁴He guided them with the cloud by day

and with light from the fire all night.
¹⁵He split the rocks in the wilderness
    and gave them water as abundant as the seas;
¹⁶he brought streams out of a rocky crag
    and made water flow down like rivers."
(Psalm 78:11–16, NIV, emphasis mine)

Many of us have seen great miracles too, but most wouldn't compare to a huge body of water drying up and dividing right in front of us. If the Israelites could forget what God did for them, we can forget as well. Because of this, we need to ask God to remind us through His written Word and by hearing His voice of all that He's done for us. He's a good Daddy, who doesn't mind reminding us 50,000,000 times! He's always patient with us and wants to help us and rescue us.

God knew we'd need help in every area of our life, including remembering His miracles, so He sent us the Holy Spirit. As believers, we have His Spirit inside us, speaking to us and reminding us of those things that'll bring us to a place of victory: "The Helper, the Holy Spirit, whom the Father will send in my name, will teach you everything and **make you remember** all that I have told you" (John 14:26, GNT, emphasis mine).

Although Psalm 103 lists many areas of benefit that the Lord has provided for us, in the remainder of this chapter, we'll focus on three: forgiveness, healing, and God's kindness.

The Benefit of Forgiveness

In Isaiah 43:25, the Lord said, "I, even I, am He Who blots out *and* cancels your transgressions, for My own sake, and **I will not remember your sins**" (AMPC, emphasis mine). And, in Psalm 103, He told us to "forget not" the benefits of forgiveness (NIV). Since God doesn't remember our sins according to Isaiah 43:25, He also wants us to forget them. We should remember the forgiveness He has provided for us, but forget about our sin. Bible teacher Andrew Wommack likes to say that when we remember the benefit of forgiveness, we'll live holier more on accident than we ever could on purpose.

We must remember that we have an enemy seeking whom he may devour (1 Peter 5:8). Also called the "accuser" in Revelation 12:10, Satan wants us to forget our forgiveness and remember our sins—just the opposite of what God wants us to do. When we remember our forgiveness, we'll manifest joy, peace, love, forgiveness toward others, love for ourselves, freedom in our relationship with the Father, and the absence of shame and condemnation. God knows that when we remember our forgiveness, we'll run to Him and not away from Him when we fail.

When we remember that God has cancelled out and paid for our sins and no longer remembers them, it enables us to forgive the wrongs that others have done to us. When we realize how much we've been forgiven, we can extend that forgiveness to others.

The Benefit of Healing

Many Christians believe that in order to realize God's benefit of healing, they must receive prayer from a big name minister. But, if the big name ministers are being truthful, they'll admit that believing this way is false because every Christian has the same authority for miraculous healings as they do. However, we must know in our heart that we have this authority because it's the truth we know that makes us free. We must know without a shadow of a doubt that healing belongs to us, His precious children. I do believe that God uses those who have the gift of healing to heal others, but His ultimate desire is for all of us to know that all of His promises and benefits belong to us because of Jesus.

For years, when I was in bondage to bipolar disorder and addictions, I didn't know that healing was mine. I thought that God healed some people but not everyone. And, I certainly didn't believe He would heal me. I begged and pleaded with Him to allow me to experience peace and healing, even though I was told that my diagnoses were incurable. The day my recovery group leader told me that nothing was impossible with God and that the enemy was trying to destroy my life, I knew right then that I could resist him and he would flee from me (James 4:7).

I knew healing was mine because of Jesus and that I needed to use my authority. I knew that, as a child of God, I didn't need to let the enemy harass and torment me any longer. After receiving the revelation that we already have healing and everything else we need the moment we say yes to Jesus, I knew that God would never withhold healing from me. I believe He's grieved when we think He withholds from us because that's never His heart. God is a giver, not a withholder.

The whole time, God was pursuing me with truth. He was pursuing me with His love, even in the midst of me getting drunk and cutting myself. I realized that I qualified for healing even when I was relapsing and suicidal. I realized that it was not my behavior that qualified me, but it was what Jesus did for me. Jesus paid the price for my healing—and yours—over 2,000 years ago. You qualify for the benefit of healing because Jesus paid for it with His stripes. It is yours! Say aloud right now, "God is not a withholder. He's my Healer. I'm already healed, and God wants me to know it and remember it."

Like the Israelites, I sometimes forget about this miraculous healing and tolerate symptoms of sickness in my body or accusing voices of condemnation. If I'm praying for others, especially those I deeply love, I have no problem remembering the benefit of healing and using my authority for them. I get mad at sickness attacking them and love to pray out of love to see them well. Yet, when it comes to me, I will sometimes tolerate or forget the benefits that belong to me. Then the Father reminds me that I'm an overcomer and how much belongs to me. I'll arise again and say, "Oh yeah, I don't have to tolerate this because Jesus already took care of it for me."

When this happens, I know that I'm receiving the Father's love, realizing that I too qualify for every promise in the Word of God. I need to immerse myself in the Word and re-read the true stories of Jesus healing all who came to Him. All means all. Acts 10:38 says, "How God anointed Jesus of Nazareth with the Holy Spirit and power, and how he went around doing good and healing all who were under the power of the devil, because God was with Him" (NIV).

Not only is healing ours, but we may be the miracle that someone else needs. It's important to understand that we're also anointed and have the Holy Spirit with us and in us. We have power over all sickness. In Matthew 10:8, Jesus told His disciples, "Heal the sick, raise the dead, cure those with leprosy, and cast out demons. Give as freely as you have received!" (NLT).

Some of you may be struggling right now, and the enemy is tempting you to give up. He tempts all of us in this way. Perhaps sickness symptoms in your body are tiring you out. The enemy wants you to forget the benefit of healing, but God wants you to remember that healing belongs to you. Don't give up! The enemy doesn't possess patience, which is a fruit of the spirit, a spiritual blessing we possess by the life of Christ in us. Patient people display endurance and perseverance. If you don't give up and continue to resist the enemy's lies, he'll eventually quit because he doesn't have patience.

Keep resisting him by remembering the truth and your benefit of healing in Christ. You will make it to the other side. You're already there in the spirit, and your body will follow the truth that you believe. Healing is yours! God's relentless, rescuing, and restoring love purchased your healing and wholeness. Believe you have received it, and walk in it.

The Benefit of God's Kindness

My greatest desire in this life is to spread the good news that God is a good God. I love talking about how good and kind and loving He is. If you follow me on Facebook, I constantly talk about His love and goodness. I'm always amazed at the positive feedback I receive just from the daily reminders of His love to others. I tell people all the time that I post those nuggets from my heart, because I also need the daily reminder of His love. I've heard people say that always talking about love is elementary and that we need to move on to higher spiritual truths. That actually makes me laugh because the most simple but profound and life-changing revelation we'll ever have is that God passionately loves us and that He is good.

If you grew up in a dysfunctional household with parents that don't know they are loved, as I did, it makes you question your worth. This is why when I discovered (and still am discovering) how much God loves me unconditionally, it radically changed my life and my relationship with Him. The Bible says that God is love (1 John 4:8). Love is who He is. Love cannot be separated from who He is. He's kind and tenderhearted, and everything He does comes from His heart of love for us. I believe we were created by love and to be loved by Him.

God is so full of love that He had to share it. He had children that He had to share His love with. He created you to share in His love for all eternity. He created you because He loves you. There's no other you. You are unique and special, and no one can take your place in the Father's heart of love.

Romans 5:1–2 tells us a little about the kindness of God:

"¹Our faith in Jesus transfers God's righteousness to us and he now declares us flawless in his eyes. This means we can now enjoy true and lasting peace with God, all because of what our Lord Jesus, the Anointed One, has done for us. ²Our faith guarantees us **permanent access into this marvelous kindness** that has given us a perfect relationship with God." (TPT, emphasis mine)

Synonyms of the word *permanent* include *stable, everlasting, invariable, changeless, continual, for keeps, forever, imperishable, in for the long haul, indestructible, set in stone, steadfast, unchanging,* and *unfading.*[1]

Synonyms for *marvelous* are *astonishing, astounding, awe-inspiring, awesome, breathtaking, extraordinary, fabulous, fantastic, incredible, miraculous, phenomenal, remarkable, spectacular, stunning, wonderful, difficult to believe, incomprehensible, staggering, surprising,* and *supernatural.*[2]

And, synonyms of *kindness* are *affection, gentleness, goodness, grace, patience, sweetness, sympathy, tenderness, unselfishness, heart,* and *kindliness.*[3]

Romans 5:1–2 with these synonyms inserted becomes:

"¹Our faith in Jesus transfers God's righteousness to us and he now declares us flawless in his eyes. This means we can now enjoy true and lasting peace with God, all because of what our Lord Jesus, the Anointed One, has done for us. ²Our faith guarantees us permanent (stable, everlasting, invariable, changeless, continual, for keeps, forever, imperishable, in for the long haul, indestructible, set in stone, steadfast, unchanging, and unfading) access into this marvelous (astonishing, astounding, awe-inspiring, awesome, breathtaking, extraordinary, fabulous, fantastic, incredible, miraculous, phenomenal, remarkable, spectacular, stunning, wonderful, difficult to believe, incomprehensible, staggering, surprising, and supernatural) kindness (affection, gentleness, goodness, grace, patience, sweetness, sympathy, tenderness, unselfishness, heart, kindliness) that has given us a perfect relationship with God."

As a child of God, we have permanent access into His marvelous kindness. When you grow up in an atmosphere of questioning your love, it takes time to renew your mind to discover that there's nothing that'll ever change God's love and kindness toward you.

I once heard that if we grow up in a very strict, legalistic household, there will sometimes be a testing season once we learn about God's grace. This happened with me. When I failed, I'd see if God's grace was really true. Would God still love me and cause good to happen in my life, regardless of my behavior, or would He treat me the way legalistic humans have? I discovered that when I failed, He loved me with His words and by showing me certain scriptures at just the right time. He also showed me feathers and certain numbers because He knew that I would understand that they were from Him.

When you receive a realization of His perfect love, it causes you to rest in it and not test it anymore, but it can be a process to get there. Give yourself grace wherever you are in the process. The voice of accusation wants us to forget that God is kind and that He works all things out for our good and never withholds any good thing from us. That lying voice of accusation wants you to think that God is mad at you when you fail and that He's going to cause bad things to happen when you mess up or get yourself into trouble. That's a lie. Even if we have earthly consequences for the messes we get ourselves into, He helps us and gets us to the other side.

God wants us to remember that we have permanent access to His marvelous kindness 24 hours a day, 7 days a week, and it's not based on our behavior but on who He is. The enemy wants us to think that God is mad at us, thinks badly about us, or is disappointed with us.

Never Forget

Jesus paid for all of our benefits listed in Psalm 103. It is finished and done! The Hebrew word for *benefits* is *gemul* and means a "benefit, recompense, or reward." It means "what is done" or "what is deserved."[4] And, *recompense* means "to pay, remunerate, to pay or give compensation for."[5]

Jesus' death and resurrection MORE THAN compensated for the damage that incurred at the fall of man when sin and death entered the world. He has satisfied every wrong and made it right at the cross. As a result of what Jesus did for us in love, He says that we deserve all of the rewards He paid for. Our faith in Jesus transfers all of the benefits to our account. His life in us is our righteousness, healing, joy, life, love, peace, and every good thing! God says, "Don't forget! Remember the benefits, My child!"

Don't forget that you're loved, healed, forgiven, righteous, in the Father's kindness and thoughts 24/7, crowned with love and mercy, royalty, and you soar like an eagle. Not only does God want us to remember our benefits, but He wants us to know that He'll never forget us:

> **Isaiah 49:15, AMP**—"[The LORD answered] 'Can a woman forget her nursing child and have no compassion on the son of her womb? Even these may forget, but **I will not forget you.**'" (emphasis mine)

When your heart hurts, He's there to help you. When you mess up, He's there to help you. When you desire growth or change and realize you can't do it, but He can, He's there to help you. He'll speak His love and grace to you, and suddenly, it doesn't seem so hard anymore. Suddenly, it doesn't feel hopeless. Suddenly, things make sense. Suddenly, your heart feels peace and joy. Suddenly, you realize you can't do it, but He can.

When your heart hurts, He's there to help you. When you mess up, He's there to help you. When you desire growth or change and realize you can't do it, but He can, He's there to help you. He'll speak His love and grace to you, and suddenly, it doesn't seem so hard anymore. Suddenly, it doesn't feel hopeless. Suddenly, things make sense. Suddenly, your heart feels peace and joy. Suddenly, you realize you can't do it, but He can.

He's an amazing Father, who knows that we'll go through trials. He'll never leave us. He'll continue to give us bear hugs of love, wisdom, life-changing truth about who we are in Him, and He'll share with us the brightness of our future and the wonderful things He has planned for us. His love for us is always consistent and never changes, and we can never be separated from it.

I encourage you to make the following declarations about yourself:

I am loved

I am forgiven

I am righteous

I am in the Father's kindness and thoughts constantly

I am crowned with love and mercy

I soar like the eagle with Jesus

I am royalty

I am precious

I am cherished

I am flawless

I am His favorite

CHAPTER 7

THE CULTURE OF HEAVEN

My husband was born in France and grew up learning its language and culture. He started studying English and eventually became a foreign exchange student at the university in Michigan where we met. When Claude came to the U.S., he was on a student visa and not considered a resident. Needing to extensively use his English skills, he was forced to grow quickly in the language. He also began to adapt to our culture, learning the rules of the land and learning about the university. Additionally, he soon discovered that Americans don't serve croissants for breakfast and have wine with every meal! And, he learned that Americans don't spend three hours at the dinner table every night; therefore, he couldn't spend three hours in the college cafeteria eating dinner because it would close.

Claude realized that he needed to learn the culture in order to succeed in the U.S. He had to learn more English to understand his classes and the people around him. If he didn't learn the language or the culture, his experience in the U.S. would've been very different, and he wouldn't have achieved his full potential. He knew he had to keep learning and growing. He eventually found a job in America and has now been immersed in our language and culture for over twenty-five years.

When Claude was still in high school in France, there was a time when he didn't do very well in his English class. His father met with Claude's teacher, along with Claude's classmates' parents. During the meeting, the teacher said publicly to Claude's dad that Claude would never do well in English. Little did he know that one day Claude would be married to an American, fluent in English, speaking to his children in English, and become a CEO of a company, speaking English to everyone! This just proves that we can't allow people's negative words over us to influence our destinies.

Claude became an American citizen in 2006 after having a student visa, a work visa, and a green card. He had to renounce his French citizenship to become American because the U.S. and France don't recognize dual citizenship. Legally, Claude is no longer considered French. He's an American citizen, entitled to all of the rights that come with that citizenship.

Claude's story reminds me of Paul's words in Colossians 1:13–14:

> "[13]For He has rescued us *and* has drawn us to Himself from the dominion of darkness, and has **transferred us to the kingdom of His beloved Son,** [14]in whom we have redemption [because of his sacrifice, resulting in] the forgiveness of our sins [and the cancellation of sins' penalty]." (AMP, emphasis mine)

Once we put our faith in Jesus, we were removed from the culture of darkness (the world) and placed in the culture (kingdom) of heaven. We don't need a temporary visa; we are permanent citizens in the kingdom of God!

Language of God's Kingdom

Just as Claude had to learn a new language when he came to America, we also have to learn a new language when we come into God's kingdom. And, just as it took time for Claude to grow in his new language of English, it will take time for us to get used to our new language because the old language of the world is all around us. It may feel unnatural at first, but the more we do it, the more we'll learn to speak positively about ourselves and others.

When you're trying to learn about the culture of another country, you research it and read about it. In the same way, we need to read and study the Word of God. It tells us who we are in Christ and how to speak our new language. As we spend time in the Word, our new identity as citizens of heaven and children of God will emerge.

While there are many aspects to our new heavenly language, we'll discuss three here: the language of gratitude, the language of righteousness, and the language of power.

Language of gratitude

Growing up, I was so used to feeling anxiety instead of peace. Even now, when everything is going well, I think, *Wait a minute! I should be stressing about something.* I was conditioned to focus on everything that was wrong instead of everything that was right.

The enemy is good at having us focus on the one thing going wrong in our lives instead of the many good things going well. Our carnal mind tends to focus on the negative, which is why we need to continually immerse ourselves in truth. When you notice yourself thinking and speaking negatively, remind yourself that you now have a new language—kingdom language. Kingdom language is a language of gratitude, even in the midst of trials. It's the opposite language of the world.

1 Thessalonians 5:18 reminds us to "give thanks in all circumstances; for this is God's will for you in Christ Jesus" (NIV). Paul showed us the language of thanksgiving and praise while he was in prison. He had been stripped and beaten with rods before being sent to prison (Acts 16:22–24), yet he didn't fall into self-pity. He didn't say, "Back in jail again! Why does this always happen to me?"

Instead, he started praising the Lord when his situation was at its worst. Then, an amazing thing happened. An earthquake shook the prison, causing the doors to open, and Paul was set free (Acts 16:22–26). This is a powerful story! God will do for you what He did for Paul. You are His child too! The Word shows us what to do and how to act like kingdom kids.

Several months ago, I was walking my dog, Rudy, a nearly thirty-pound Sheltie. At the beginning of our walk, it was nice outside, and everything was going smoothly. Nearing the end of our walk, however, it started pouring down rain. I tried to stop under a tree with Rudy, but he wasn't having it. I had to pick him up and run home with him. He was heavy, and we were both getting soaked.

In that moment, I could've chosen to become bitter and thought, *It figures! I'm tired of having to walk dogs. Why does this always happen to me? Now I have to do my hair all over again.* Instead, I knew I had a choice and decided to start saying aloud, "Thank You, Father, that I live in this neighborhood. Thank You for the gift of Rudy. Thank You that I'm healthy and able to walk him, even in the rain."

I don't always respond with such gratitude, but I'm growing more and more in learning to respond as a kingdom citizen with the kingdom language of gratitude. Sometimes we have to make the choice: Are we going to respond like the world to negative situations, or are we going to respond like loved, forgiven, righteous, and grateful children of God?

Language of righteousness

Our enemy, the devil, has a language too. One aspect of his language is accusation. Revelation 12:10 calls him the "accuser of the brethren." When he starts shouting his accusing voice at you, telling you that you're a failure as a mom, you aren't good enough, you aren't taking care of your body, you're an angry person, or you don't know how to forgive, don't agree with his voice.

That language belongs to the old you, not the new you. You've been transferred from the kingdom of darkness (the devil's kingdom) into the kingdom of heaven (the kingdom of God's Son). This isn't your language anymore. Your new language is one of righteousness in Christ.

What does our language of righteousness sound like? Whenever you fail, you can remind yourself, "I'm righteous because of Jesus. I'm forgiven. He no longer sees me with failures. I'm loved, and

I'm accepted." When you use your language of righteousness in the midst of failure or when those voices of accusation come, it will help you remember the truth about your identity, which will help you through mistakes or struggles. The language of righteousness remembers that there's no barrier between us and our good Father, and absolutely nothing can separate us from His love.

Along with knowing our righteousness, we must also understand that we're totally complete because of Jesus. Colossians 2:10 tells us, "And in Him you have been made complete [achieving spiritual stature through Christ], and He is the head over all rule and authority [of every angelic and earthly power]" (AMP).

Just as he did to Eve in the Garden of Eden, the devil likes to tell us that we still need something besides Jesus, as if He alone isn't enough. He wants us to believe that God is holding out on us and that there's more we need in order to be content. This is the language of the world—always achieving and striving, yet never satisfied. But, the language of God's kingdom says, "You are complete in Jesus, and because of Him, you have everything you'll ever need. Stop striving, and rest in Me."

Language of power

We can belong to the kingdom of heaven and never learn the language, the culture, and our rights as heavenly citizens. As discussed in the last chapter, when we receive Jesus, we also receive a benefits package that includes resurrection power to move mountains, change situations, and change the world. We have a new language of power and love. We are now bulletproof in the spirit, and when weapons come against us, we can speak out our new heavenly language against them:

Isaiah 54:17, AMP—"No weapon that is formed against you will succeed; and every tongue that rises against you in judgment *you will condemn.* This [peace, righteousness, security, and triumph over opposition] is the heritage of the servants of the LORD, and *this is* their vindication from Me," says the LORD." (emphasis mine)

Notice this verse says, "you will condemn." If you're hit with pain symptoms in your body, you can "condemn" those symptoms by speaking the opposite truth, which is that you're healed because of Jesus. If you have relational issues with someone, you can speak restoration and reconciliation. We're full of the resurrection power of Jesus, which makes us powerful and not powerless. If you've been given an incurable diagnosis, and the doctors cannot help you, you're in a great place to receive the healing power of Jesus that belongs to you.

We live in this earthly world, but we've been transferred spiritually into the kingdom of heaven, so we're called to live and speak differently than the world speaks. When the enemy comes your way, you can boldly say, "Is that all you got for me?" instead of cowering in fear. Jesus equipped you with everything you'll ever need to live victoriously. Never lose the wonder of what Jesus did for you. You are full of power, and there's power in your words when they line up with God's Word.

Overpowering Fear

Even though we have God's power, we may often feel powerless. This is due to fear, which is the opposite of faith. We must keep our eyes on Jesus, and remember the truth of who we are in the face of fear:

Isaiah 54:14, AMP—"You will be firmly established in righteousness: You will be far from [even the thought of] oppression, for you will not fear, and from terror, for it will not come near you."

When we're firmly established in our right standing with God, it causes us to be far from even the thought of oppression, and we will not fear. Speak truth in the face of fear. We have resurrection power in us, but sometimes we have to let it out! Speaking truth in the face of fear comes from a place of rest, knowing our identity and understanding that we're secure in His perfect love.

If you came home one day and found a stranger in your house eating your food, watching your TV, and sitting in your favorite chair, would you just let that person do as he or she wanted? No, everything in you would yell, "Get out of my house! You don't belong there!" You might also call the police, who would use their authority to capture the intruder. In the same way, you've been delegated the authority of Jesus Christ to capture and get rid of those intruders that try to steal, kill, and destroy your life.

You have the power to focus on thoughts of peace instead of thoughts of fear. You can do it because you are powerful and not powerless. Our new kingdom language says, "nothing is impossible," "nothing is incurable," and "I can do all things through Christ." I encourage you to find other powerful life-changing truths from the Word to dwell on when thoughts of doubt, negativity, and fear come your way. The Word will literally transfer you from fear to peace because it's a powerful weapon:

Hebrews 4:12, NIV—"For the word of God is alive and active. Sharper than any double-edged sword, it penetrates even to dividing soul and spirit, joints and marrow...."

Sin and Forgiveness in God's Kingdom

God views us as if we never sinned. Second Corinthians 5:21 explains, "He made Christ who knew no sin to [judicially] be sin on our behalf, so that in Him we would become the righteousness of God [that is, we would be made acceptable to Him and placed in a right relationship with Him by His gracious lovingkindness]" (AMP).

When God looks at the sacrifice of Jesus, He says, "It is good, it is finished. My children are righteous. My children are clean, pure, holy, and forgiven." You are a radically loved, forgiven, and righteous child of God. It takes a revelation of the Holy Spirit to know this because this world operates in a completely opposite manner.

For example, many celebrities in the public eye have had great accomplishments in their field and are known and idolized for this. Yet, as soon as they have a public failure, they're typically shunned and only remembered for that failure. I'm not condoning sin in any way, but I have compassion on people because I know what I've been delivered of, and I realize that people do things because of their hurt and the lies they've believed. They don't know they're forgiven and loved by a good Father. Everyone needs Jesus!

The kingdom of God is opposite of the world's kingdom. God removed our sin and remembers it no more. We children of God must be an example to those around us and look at others through God's eyes, knowing that "but for the grace of God go I." If Jesus didn't go to the cross, we'd all be doomed.

James 2:10 says, "For the person who keeps all of the laws except one is as guilty as a person who has broken all of God's laws" (NLT). There aren't levels of sin in God's eyes because Jesus became sin and removed it all as far as the east is from the west. There are different consequences for sin here on earth, but we are kingdom children, who are called to live differently than the world.

If you've been wronged, try to view the person who wronged you through the eyes of radical love, just as the Father does with us. Ask God to help you see people through His eyes, and He will. He'll help you extend forgiveness and to see others in their true identity. Forgiveness, however, doesn't automatically bring trust back into a relationship.

Psychologist and author Dr. Henry Cloud explains:

> "Differentiating between forgiveness and trust does a number of things. First, you prevent the other person from being able to say that not opening up again means you are 'holding it against me.' Second, you draw a clear

line from the past to the possibility of a good future with a new beginning point of today, with a new plan and new expectations...."[1]

Trust can often be re-established in relationships. However, if a person proves to be untrustworthy over and over again, you may decide that you need to move on from that relationship in order to keep your peace. Ask the Father for wisdom about the situation, and He'll give it to you because He's a good Father.

The Kingdom of Love

When we were translated from the kingdom of this world to the kingdom of Christ, we received a new Father—a good, heavenly Father:

> **Galatians 3:26, AMP**—"For you [who are born-again have been reborn from above—spiritually transformed, renewed, sanctified and] are all children of God [set apart for His purpose with full rights and privileges] through faith in Christ Jesus."

Our Father has always loved us and longed for us to be in His kingdom. In Jeremiah 31:3, God told His people, "I've never quit loving you and never will. Expect love, love, and more love" (MSG).

Being transferred into God's kingdom means that we're now never alone. We'll always be cared for. We're loved, safe, and secure with Him. He sees us only with eyes of pure love. He reminds us to relax when we feel anxious, and He reminds us that He's in control. He can never love us any more than He does, and He'll never love us any less.

Romans 8:38–39 reminds us that we can never be separated from His relentless, rescuing, and restoring love:

> "³⁸So now I live with the confidence that there is nothing in the universe with the power to separate us from God's love. I'm convinced that his love will triumph over death, life's troubles, fallen angels, or dark rulers in the heavens. There is nothing in our present or future circumstances that can weaken his love. ³⁹There is no power above us or beneath us—no power that could ever be found in the universe that can distance us from God's passionate love, which is lavished upon us through our Lord Jesus, the Anointed One!" (TPT)

In the world, people will leave us, betray us, reject us, and hurt us. We will get hurt. Yet, we can have confidence that the loving God of the universe will never do these things to us. When we understand His love for us, we can get through any painful trial that may come our way. Remind yourself often that you can never be separated from God's love.

Before moving on to Chapter 8, declare the following:

I am forgiven

I am loved

I am righteous

I am complete

I am a radically loved child of God

I have a new Father

I am His favorite

I am healed

I am powerful, not powerless

I have the authority of Jesus to move mountains

I am an overcomer

CHAPTER 8

THE HEALER OF BROKEN HEARTS

We were never created to live with a broken heart. That was never God's plan. The fall of man brought with it a big list of problems we were never meant to go through. God knew that some of the tragedies and traumas we'd experience would cause us emotional pain or break our hearts in some way.

We need to know His heart for us when we experience pain and trauma. We need to know that we have a Father who cares about what we go through, never leaves us, and has provided healing in the atonement for our broken hearts.

Jesus literally died of a broken heart. In addition to everything we learned about in Chapter 1, which Jesus experienced during crucifixion, His heart actually ripped inside His chest as He hung on the cross. When the soldiers stuck the spear in His side to see if He was still alive, water and blood came gushing forth. Medical doctors have said this is indicative of His heart being torn.[1] Jesus' broken heart and broken body paid the price so we won't have to live with brokenness.

We don't have to live our whole lives with a broken heart if we receive His healing. Jesus is the Healer of broken hearts, broken relationships, broken emotions, and broken homes. He was broken so we could be free, healed, and whole in every area of our lives.

John wrote in his gospel that we will have trials in this life, but Jesus has overcome the world (16:33). Jesus is the answer. This verse never says that God causes our trials, because He doesn't. If we believe that God is the one causing bad things to happen to us, we'll never run to Him for help.

But, even though we're promised trials, the good news is that we're also promised all of God's benefits and help when we go through hurt, pain, and trauma. In this chapter, we'll focus on three promises that God has given us when we're suffering from a broken heart or any other brokenness in our lives: (1) Jesus came to heal broken hearts; (2) our Father has compassion on the hurting; and (3) we are one with Jesus' authoritative power.

Jesus Came to Heal Broken Hearts

One of the primary reasons Jesus came to earth was to heal broken hearts. Jesus told us to not let our hearts be troubled and to not be afraid (John 14:27), but He knew that many of us would fail in this from time to time. First, we need to come to a place of peace after our heart is healed, and then we must learn how to give our future cares and concerns to Him.

Jesus said about Himself in Isaiah 61:1,

> "The Spirit of the Lord GOD is upon me,
> Because the LORD has anointed *and* commissioned me
> To bring good news to the humble *and* afflicted;

He has sent me to **bind up [the wounds of] the brokenhearted,**
To proclaim release [from confinement and condemnation] to the [physical and spiritual] captives
And freedom to prisoners...." (AMP, emphasis mine)

"The Spirit of GOD, the Master, is on me
    because GOD anointed me.
He sent me to preach good news to the poor,
    heal the heartbroken,
Announce freedom to all captives,
    pardon all prisoners." (MSG, emphasis mine)

The Hebrew word for *brokenhearted* in this verse is *shabar*, which means "to break, break in pieces."[2] Jesus knew that our heart would sometimes break, and He didn't want us to live with a broken heart, so He came to heal us. NASB translations of *brokenhearted* are *crushed, demolished, destroy, fractured, injured, shattered,* and *torn down.*[3]

If you feel you have a crushed, demolished, destroyed, fractured, injured, shattered, or torn down heart in some area, don't give up hope. Jesus is your answer. He came to heal you and set you free. He'll reveal to you anything you're holding on to that needs to be released to Him.

Notice when Jesus read this Isaiah 61 passage in the synagogue, which pointed to Him being the Messiah (also quoted in Luke 4:17–21), healing the brokenhearted is listed second after preaching the good news. I believe that "bring good news to the poor" is listed first because the more we meditate on what Jesus did for us—forgiving us, healing us, loving us, making us righteous by faith, adopting us as His precious children, saving us, giving us eternal life, and coming to dwell in us—we'll understand that this is what cures and completely heals our broken heart and losses.

In addition, Isaiah 61:1 applies to us in the same manner that it applies to Jesus. We're anointed to preach the good news and heal the brokenhearted just as Jesus was. This is why it's important to get our own heart healed, so we can then go heal the world. But even in our brokenness or wrong believing, we can still heal others because it's not about us; it's about Jesus. I've been healing from a broken heart recently, yet I've still seen people get healed through my ministry because it's not about me. Ultimately, however, Jesus wants us to walk in complete healing and wholeness, and He wants us to desire it for ourselves as much as we want it for others.

The journey of healing

There are many traumatic events in life that may lead to a broken heart, such as having a spouse leave for another man or woman, having a loved one die unexpectedly, car accidents or other incidents resulting in physical injury, getting fired from a job, being unable to have children, losing a child, or betrayal. Other events could be added to this list, but regardless of the cause, if we don't get our heart healed, it can rob us of life.

Jesus came to give us an abundant life, and He wants us to live in joy and peace, no matter what comes our way. He's with us in our healing journey as we allow Him to heal every piece of our shattered heart. Then we can live again and experience His love, joy, peace, and all the good plans He has for our lives. Proverbs 13:12 tells us that hope deferred makes our heart sick. Jesus came to restore hope in every area of our lives.

For many, heartbreak stems from a place deep in childhood, which is where mine began. Children are never meant to experience verbal, physical, or sexual abuse, or be thrown against walls, abandoned, and treated as inferiors. But, that was my entire childhood. I had a reason to feel broken. In fact, living with a broken heart was more normal for me than having peace. (You can learn more about my childhood and how God healed my broken heart in my book, *Hold On to Hope*.)

As an adult, because I hadn't yet received healing for my heart, I believe that my childhood trauma manifested in my physical body as endometriosis and in my brain as mental illness. The endometriosis produced much pain physically, and then later, mental illness manifested as bipolar disorder and addictions, among other things.

Because I didn't know where to go with my pain, I tried to fill the void and remove the pain with substance addictions. As I received the truth of my real identity in Christ and came to know Jesus as Healer over twelve years ago, much instant healing occurred. I've been free from bipolar, addictions, and endometriosis since that time, and in those twelve years, God had to heal my broken heart over issues for which I was grieving.

Healing is always what God desires for us, whether it's instant or progressive. And, if it is progressive, that's okay. As stated earlier, process is not a bad thing. As I meditated on the Word of God, walked alongside some wonderful people, and heard my Father's voice instead of the voice of accusation, much healing has taken place in my heart. I had to give myself grace during my journey, and I encourage you to do the same. I'm not where I was ten years ago, five years ago, or even a year ago. Rejoice over any growth or healing in your life. It's cause for celebration!

Learning to replace deeply rooted lies with the truth of Jesus being my foundation has radically changed my life. Jesus came to give us life, but the enemy comes to steal, kill, and destroy (John 10:10). The enemy's goal is to make us feel defective and worthless. He wants us to think we don't matter and that we're a mistake and a failure. He wants us to take our eyes off the truth of who God says we are.

When those voices of accusation come, fight against them by saying, "God, You say I'm worthy, blameless, flawless, beautiful, forgiven, righteous, loved, and Your precious child, who you cherish. You say that I can never be separated from Your love. You say that I'm not a failure, but I'm victorious because of Jesus."

Our good Father loves us so much. He doesn't want us to have any brokenness in our lives. He wants us to be whole. We're complete in Him, whether we feel it or not. He wants us to experience His peace that surpasses all understanding. We can draw on His love, peace, and anything we need by reminding ourselves and meditating on the fact that we have them all because of His life in us.

If our heart doesn't get healed, it can affect our relationships and other areas of our life. If this is happening to you, and you believe that people are leaving you, or you're angry when you know that's not who you really are, you need to stop condemning yourself. Otherwise, you'll stay in the cycle of brokenness and anger. The anger you have against yourself will lash out at others.

God wants you to give yourself grace, receive His love, and know that you're not defective. We all act outside of our true identity at times. Forgive yourself, take your wounded heart to your Father, remind yourself of your true identity, and ask Him to help you. Today may be the day you decide that you're done living with a broken heart. Keep giving yourself grace and meditating on how loved you are, and I promise you'll see changes occurring effortlessly. If it can happen for me, it can happen for anyone.

Our Father Has Compassion for the Hurting

In 1987, a young girl named Jessica McClure fell down a well, riveting the whole country to their televisions as rescuers worked day and night to get her out. Her entire community pulled together to save her. Paramedics, various experts, and contractors worked hand in hand to figure out how to drill a tunnel that would reach her. When she was finally pulled from the well alive, America rejoiced! Everyone wanted to see her safely back home.

In your own life, have you ever felt like you've fallen into a pit? Have you ever felt as if there was no way out, and you were paralyzed with hurt and fear and brokenness? Most likely, you've experienced a broken heart at least once in your life. We can all relate to falling into a pit at some point. If mankind sees a person who has fallen into a well and will do anything to rescue that person, how much more do you think our good Father has compassion on you when you feel you're so broken that there's no way out of your mess?

Matthew 12:9–13 demonstrates our Father's heart of compassion. In verse 11, the Pharisees tried to find fault with Jesus for healing on the Sabbath. Jesus asked them, "If any of you has a sheep and it falls into a pit on the Sabbath, will you not take hold of it and lift it out?" (NIV). When you're hurting or feel like you're stuck in a pit, our good Father has one goal: to come to your rescue. He doesn't condemn you while you're in the pit. His heart is for your total healing and restoration. He's a God of love and compassion. You were created by Him, and you were created to be loved by Him. That's why you're here.

When we can understand that we were created to be loved and cherished by God, it changes our whole world for the better. He wants that to be a foundational truth we believe. God is a rescuing Father who is always good and always hears our cries for help.

The following scriptures further portray the heart of our Father:

Psalm 34:17–18, MSG—
"¹⁷Is anyone crying for help? GOD is listening,
   ready to rescue you.
¹⁸If your heart is broken, you'll find GOD right there;
   if you're kicked in the gut, he'll help you catch your
   breath."

Psalm 56:8–9, TPT—

"⁸You've stored my many tears in your bottle—not one
   will be lost.
   For they are all recorded in your book of
   remembrance.
⁹The very moment I call to you for a father's help
   the tide of battle turns and my enemies flee."

Psalm 147:3, TPT—

"He heals the wounds of every shattered heart."
(emphasis mine)

Isaiah 49:13, 15–16, MSG—

"¹³GOD has comforted his people.
      He has tenderly nursed his beaten-up, beaten-
      down people.
   ¹⁵**I'd never forget you—never.**
¹⁶Look, I've written your names on the backs of my
   hands."
(emphasis mine)

Isaiah 54:10, NIV—

"Though the mountains be shaken
   and the hills be removed,
yet my **unfailing love for you** will not be shaken
   nor my covenant of peace be removed,"
      says the LORD, **who has compassion on you."**
(emphasis mine)

Zephaniah 3:17, MSG—
"…he'll **calm you** with his love and **delight you** with his songs." (emphasis mine)

Hebrews 13:5, AMP—
"…for He has said, 'I WILL NEVER [under any circumstances] DESERT YOU [nor give you up nor leave you without support, nor will I in any degree leave you helpless], NOR WILL I FORSAKE *or* LET YOU DOWN *or* RELAX MY HOLD ON YOU [assuredly not]!'"

James 5:11, MSG—
"That's because God cares, cares right down to the last detail."

Most of you are probably familiar with the story of Lazarus being raised from the dead (John 11). When Jesus arrived in the town where Lazarus was buried, Mary, Martha, and the Jews who had gone to meet Him were all weeping. Upon seeing them, Jesus wept as well (John 11:35). In Bible scholar Kenneth Wuest's *The New Testament*, he translates this verse as "Jesus burst into tears and wept silently."[4] Wow! The Savior of the world cared so much about those around Him that He met them in their moment of grief.

This is reminiscent of Paul's instruction in Romans 12:15, "Rejoice with those who rejoice [sharing others' joy], and weep with those who weep [sharing others' grief]" (AMP). Jesus could've raised Lazarus from the dead immediately instead of weeping with the others. He had the solution to their grief, yet He wept with love and compassion when He saw Mary and

Martha brokenhearted over their brother's death. Jesus met them right where they were.

Jesus cares deeply for us. He cares for you and loves you in the middle of your grieving or any pit into which you may fall. He'll rescue you as many times as you need rescuing. Will you let Him rescue you? I encourage you to say yes by surrendering your cares and anxieties to Him. Listen for His voice to give you wisdom to know what to do. He knows exactly what you need before you need it, and He's provided the solution before you even encountered your problem. Right at this very moment, He's working good in whatever situation you're facing.

God never causes tragedies or bad things to happen, but He can work good out of anything. Recently, I was talking to Him about an ongoing situation in my life, and I said, "Father, I have no idea how You can work any good from this situation." He immediately responded, "Watch Me!" That was all I needed to hear, and I can't wait for an amazing outcome of good. He'll do the same for you!

We Are One with Jesus' Authoritative Power

Because we, as believers, are one with Jesus, we're also one with His authoritative power to receive healing for ourselves and to heal others, which includes both emotional and physical healing. It's His power in us that heals, and not our own power. Yet, we have a choice on whether we draw on His healing power for ourselves and others.

Throughout Jesus' earthly ministry, He showed us the heart of His Father, and He delegated to us the authority that His Father gave Him.

> **Acts 10:38, NLT**—"And you know that God anointed Jesus of Nazareth with the Holy Spirit and with **power.** Then Jesus went around doing good and healing all who were oppressed by the devil, for God was with him." (emphasis mine)

The Greek word for *healing* in this verse is *iaomai*, which means "to heal, make whole, cure."[5] Jesus went around doing good and curing people. Nothing is incurable with Jesus!

Also, the word *oppressed* in Greek is *katadunasteuo*, meaning "to exercise dominion against."[6] In the *NAS Exhaustive Concordance*, this word means "to exercise power over."[7]

Acts 10:38 says that Jesus came and did good and healed all who were being bullied by the devil. He came to set free all those who were being dominated by the enemy. The enemy oppresses us by deceiving us into believing his lies instead of God's truth. The devil is called "the father of lies" in John 8:44. He tries to make us doubt what God says in His Word.

I believe that many of those whom Jesus set free were oppressed because they experienced heartache and trauma and lost all hope for their circumstances ever changing. But, our hero, Jesus, came to rescue the captives and set them free. He came to love hurting people who were considered sinners and outcasts. His relentless, rescuing, restoring love sets people free!

No one is an outcast to Jesus. We're all precious and treasured and cherished by our good Father. Declare aloud right now, "I am treasured and cherished by my good Father. I matter to Him. I am loved by Him at this moment. It's not a future, cleaned-up version of me He loves, but He loves me right now where I am."

In Luke 10:19, Jesus told His disciples, "I have given you authority to trample on snakes and scorpions and to overcome all the **power** of the enemy; nothing will harm you" (NIV, emphasis mine).

The Greek word for *power* in Acts 10:38 and in Luke 10:19 is *dynamei*.[8] Take a moment to re-read both of these verses. Acts 10:38 refers to the power Jesus exercised on earth, and in Luke 10:19, Jesus gave His disciples (which includes us) the exact same power to heal and set the oppressed free.

This means that, as a child of God, you have the exact same power as Jesus inside of you to use for yourself and those in need of healing or deliverance. That's good news! We have authority over that father of lies, the devil. We have more authority in our pinky than he has in his whole kingdom. If we have the same power as Jesus over the enemy and sickness, how much power do they have over us? None! Zero! Zilch! Think about that.

This is a life-changing revelation that altered everything for me. When I realized the enemy was coming to steal, kill, oppress, and destroy my life, and I understood that I was a child of God with authority, I was completely set free from bipolar disorder. We have the same power as Jesus, and we are one with His authoritative power to heal.

As mentioned earlier, the devil oppresses us when we believe his lies. But he can also oppress or bully us when we hold on to unforgiveness, offense, bitterness, anger, and jealousy. And, he can oppress us through lingering sickness. Even so, we have the power to say, "I might be feeling excruciating pain right now, but I know it's leaving because it doesn't belong to me. I might have to cry in Jesus' arms, and I may have to yell and scream into a pillow because of betrayal, but I'm not staying in this pain and heartbreak. I'll grieve for a time, but Jesus is with me, and He's taking me to the other side, just as He did with the disciples in the boat when the storm came."

2 Corinthians 2:14, AMPC—
"But thanks be to God, Who in Christ **always leads us** in triumph [as trophies of Christ's victory] and through us spreads *and* makes evident the fragrance of the knowledge of God everywhere." (emphasis mine)

We are always triumphant in Christ!

Healing Through Relationship

The best way for me to receive healing of a broken heart has been through my relationship with God. Learning to know Him as my Father, hearing His voice speak to my heart, and allowing Him to lead and guide me has provided the greatest healing imaginable. I've found it to be a never-ending fun adventure discovering God's love for me through His Word. He's a Father who loves us and promises to never leave us, especially in our messes and brokenness.

2 Thessalonians 2:16–17, NASB—

"[16]Now may our Lord Jesus Christ Himself and God our Father, who has loved us and given us eternal comfort and good hope by grace, [17]comfort and strengthen your hearts in every good work and word."

The Greek word for *comfort* in verse 16 is *paraklesis*, which means "to call to one's aid, encouragement."[9] That word comes from *parakaleo*, meaning "to call for, invite."[10]

We have a Father who invites us to draw near to Him. We're one with Him, and nothing will change that. We can't get any closer to His presence by being one with Him, but we can get closer to Him in relationship by spending time getting to know Him. There are many believers who have become one with Him, yet never acknowledge His existence.

God will continually speak to people, even if they don't know that He's the one speaking. He never stops pursuing people with His love. I believe His greatest desire is that we'd get to know His true, loving nature. He wants us to know how special we are to Him and how loved we are. He's a relational God. The more we get to know Him personally by spending time with Him and His Word, the more effortlessly we'll receive His love, comfort, healing, and truth.

Those who feel their hearts have been shattered need to know who God is and how He sees them in their messes or pain. Otherwise, they'll run from Him instead of toward Him. He wants us to run to Him and His throne of grace, especially in our time of need (Hebrews 4:16). He's our answer, and He has what we need. He never wants us to hide from Him. He wants us to know that there's absolutely no barrier between Him and us.

We can always approach the Lord with our deepest secrets, and He'll never tell anyone. He wants us to learn to trust Him. People who have a childhood filled with trauma and brokenness find it hard to trust. Sometimes this mistrust is transferred to God. It takes time to learn to trust again, and He understands. He'll help you get there whenever you need it.

> **Matthew 11:28–30, AMP—**
> "²⁸Come to Me, all who are weary and heavily burdened [by religious rituals that provide no peace], and I will give you rest [refreshing your souls with salvation]. ²⁹Take My yoke upon you and learn from Me [following Me as My disciple], for I am gentle and humble in heart, and YOU WILL FIND REST (renewal, blessed quiet) FOR YOUR SOULS. ³⁰For My yoke is easy [to bear] and My burden is light."

The definition of *come* in verse 28 is "to advance, approach, or move toward something; to journey to a vicinity with a specified purpose."[11] Maybe your specified request when you come to Him is to heal your broken heart. He'll love you and show you the truth that you're one with His healing. He'll help you see that everything you need is there in Him. It'll awaken you as you believe it, and it'll manifest in your heart and in your body.

Philippians 4:6–7 tells us, "⁶Do not be anxious about anything, but in every situation, by prayer and petition, with thanksgiving, present your requests to God. ⁷And the peace of God, which transcends all understanding, will guard your hearts and your minds in Christ Jesus" (NIV).

Maybe some of you, like me, have lived in chaos and hurt and turmoil for so long, it's more normal for you to feel restlessness or anxiety than to feel peace. Although I have been healed for nearly thirteen years, there are still times when anxiety tries to creep into my life. But, then I remember that I don't have to live in turmoil anymore because peace is my new home.

The Father wants you to know that you'll get where you need to be. He'll help you and give you rest. He promises us rest and peace. It's ours for the taking. The more we acknowledge Him and get to know Him, the more victory and healing we'll walk in that's already been given to us in Jesus.

If you're feeling brokenhearted, I encourage you to say this prayer, adding your own words if you'd like:

Father, I thank You that You sent Your precious Son, Jesus, to set me free and heal every area of my life, including my shattered heart. Help me forgive those who have hurt me and to see them through Your eyes of love. Thank You, Father, for helping me know, experience, and receive in a deeper way, the never-ending love You have for me. Thank You for reminding me who I am and how You see me as Your precious and treasured child, every moment of every day, even when I'm hurting or when I fail.

Father, I thank You that I'm being transformed by Your love every day, and I'm continually growing more and more. Help me remember to celebrate the victories. Right now, I receive Your healing for my heart. I thank You that Your healing power is flowing into my heart and every cell of my body, healing me emotionally and physically. Thank You for Your broken body that has set me free. I love You, Father. Thank You for choosing me to be Your child. In Jesus' precious name I pray. Amen.

CONCLUSION

I want to conclude this book with another reminder that we are so very loved by a good Father, no matter what. As I have stated throughout this book, I believe that it's in times of failure when we need to remember this truth the most. He wants to show us that nothing changes His love for us, and He wants to love us to freedom and wholeness.

I recently began studying the Prodigal Son parable found in the Gospel of Luke. Jesus told this parable after the Pharisees complained because He was spending time with sinners. Much could be said about this parable, but I want to focus on the Father's heart in the midst of this son's failure.

Luke 15:11–32, TPT—
The Loving Father
"¹¹Then Jesus said, 'Once there was a father with two sons. ¹²The younger son came to his father and said, "Father, don't you think it's time to give me the share of your estate that belongs to me?" So the father went ahead and distributed among the two sons their inheritance. ¹³Shortly afterward, the younger son packed up all his belongings and traveled off to see the world. He journeyed to a far-off land where he soon wasted all he was given in a binge of extravagant and reckless living.

¹⁴With everything spent and nothing left, he grew hungry, for there was a severe famine in that land. ¹⁵So he begged a farmer in that country to hire him. The farmer hired him and sent him out to feed the pigs. ¹⁶The son was so famished, he was willing to even eat the slop given to the pigs, because no one would feed him a thing.

¹⁷Humiliated, the son finally realized what he was doing and he thought, "There are many workers at my father's house who have all the food they want with plenty to spare. They lack nothing. Why am I here dying of hunger, feeding these pigs and eating their slop? ¹⁸I want to go back home to my father's house, and I'll say to him, 'Father, I was wrong. I have sinned against you. ¹⁹I'll never be worthy to be called your son. Please, Father, just treat me like one of your employees.'"

²⁰So the young son set off for home. From a long distance away, his father saw him coming, *dressed as a beggar*, and great compassion swelled up in his heart for his son who was returning home. So the father raced out to meet him. He swept him up in his arms, hugged him dearly, and kissed him over and over with tender love.

²¹Then the son said, "Father, I was wrong. I have sinned against you. I could never deserve to be called your son. Just let me be—" The father interrupted and said, "Son, you're home now!"

²²Turning to his servants, the father said, "Quick, bring me the best robe, my very own robe, and I will place it on his shoulders. Bring the ring, the seal of sonship, and I will put it on his finger. And bring out the best shoes you can find for my son. ²³Let's *prepare a great feast* and

celebrate. [24]For this beloved son of mine was once dead, but now he's alive again. Once he was lost, but now he is found!" And everyone celebrated with overflowing joy.

[25]Now, the older son was out working in the field when his brother returned, and as he approached the house he heard the music of celebration and dancing. [26]So he called over one of the servants and asked, "What's going on?"

[27]The servant replied, "It's your younger brother. He's returned home and your father is throwing a party to celebrate his homecoming."

[28]The older son became angry and refused to go in and celebrate. So his father came out and pleaded with him, "Come and enjoy the feast with us!"

[29]The son said, "Father, listen! How many years have I been working like a slave for you, performing every duty you've asked as a faithful son? And I've never once disobeyed you. But you've never thrown a party for me because of my faithfulness. Never once have you even given me a goat that I could feast on and celebrate with my friends like he's doing now. [30]But look at this son of yours! He comes back after wasting your wealth on prostitutes and reckless living, and here you are throwing a great feast to celebrate—for him!"

[31]The father said, "My son, you are always with me by my side. Everything I have is yours to enjoy. [32]It's only right to celebrate like this and be overjoyed, because this brother of yours was once dead and gone, but now he is alive and back with us again. He was lost but now he is found!""""

Like me, some of you may have grown up with fathers who would not have run out to meet you and kiss you when you failed. Instead, they'd run out to yell at you and possibly beat you or throw you out of the family. But, our heavenly Father is a good Father, and we're completely safe with Him.

In an sermon titled "Prodigal Love for the Prodigal Son," Charles Spurgeon explained that the word *kiss* in Luke 15:20 is translated "and kissed him much" or "kissed him eagerly and earnestly."[1]

The father couldn't wait to kiss his son, so he ran toward him. He didn't wait for his son to come to him. Author Matt Williams wrote that, in first-century culture, a man would never run. If he were to run, he would have to pull up his tunic to keep from tripping on it. It was considered shameful for a man to show his bare legs. Also in those days, if a Jewish son lost his inheritance to the Gentiles, when he returned home, his family and community would have a ceremony and break a large pot in front of him. They'd then tell him that he was now cut off from his people, and he was rejected by his community.

Williams goes on to say that the father ran to the son, not wanting him to experience humiliation and shame from the community. The father wanted to reach his son before anyone else did. He wanted to take the shame for his son and show him that he was welcome at home, and he wouldn't be rejected.[2]

I believe this is a picture of Jesus taking our shame at the cross. He took our every sin and failure, so the Father no longer sees us with sin or failure, only passionate love. Our good Father runs after us with His relentless, rescuing, and restoring love.

He kisses us, loves on us, and shows us nothing has changed. He'll never reject us or change His loving view of us. When you fail and want to condemn yourself, remember that there's no condemnation for you, only love.

When you feel far off, the Father never stops looking at you with eyes of love ready to restore you and help you. He'll never kick you out of the family. You're safe with Him in His arms of love forever. He wants you to run to Him and not hide because He's always running after you to love you.

Jesus was our great Rescuer, but we have a Father who continues to rescue us in our everyday lives. He's our Helper and our Comforter, who is very relational and never distant. He's the God who kisses and gives bear hugs of love.

Never forget Jeremiah's words, and receive them for yourself today:

"God told them, 'I've never quit loving you and never will.
Expect love, love, and more love!'"
(Jeremiah 31:3, MSG)

PRAYER OF SALVATION

Heavenly Father, I believe that Jesus Christ is Your Son and that He took my place and died for my sins. I believe that on the third day, He was raised from the dead so that I could have eternal life and right standing with You. Thank You, Jesus, for taking my punishment for sin and making peace with the Father on my behalf. At this very moment, I choose to make Jesus the Savior and Lord of my life. I repent (change my mind) and turn from my past into a new future with You. I go forward now as Your child, with You as my Father, and with heaven as my home.

According to Your Word in Romans 10:9–10, I am now born again. I am a new creation in Christ (2 Corinthians 5:17). Thank You for viewing me as if I never sinned. Nothing can remove me from this place of right standing with You. Thank You that Your life is in me at this very moment, and Your Holy Spirit will continue to work out victory in every area of my life as I continue to seek You and depend on You. I will never be the same again. In Jesus' name, I pray. Amen.

Congratulations! Heaven's angels are rejoicing with you (Luke 15:10). The Father, Son, and Holy Spirit are celebrating and throwing a party just for you. Welcome into the family of God's kingdom!

If you prayed this prayer for the first time, please contact me at www.nicholemarbach.com. I would like to personally welcome you into God's family.

NOTES

Chapter 1

1. *Webster's New World College Dictionary*, 4th ed. (Boston, MA: Houghton Mifflin Harcourt, 2001), s.v. "Gethsemane."

2. *Merriam-Webster Online*, s.v. "hematidrosis," http://www.merriam-webster.com/medical/hematidrosis.

3. Frederick T. Zugibe, *The Crucifixion of Jesus: A Forensic Inquiry* (New York, NY: M. Evans and Company, Inc., 2005), pp. 13–14.

4. M.G. Easton, *Easton's Illustrated Bible Dictionary*, 3rd ed. (Scotland, UK: Thomas Nelson, 1897), s.v. "Barabbas."

5. Zugibe, p. 22.

6. Ibid, p. 36.

7. Andrew Wommack, "The War Is Over—Sin Is No Longer an Issue with God," *Gospel Truth Magazine*, Anniversary Issue 2008, p. 7.

8. Dictionary.com Unabridged, based on the *Random House Unabridged Dictionary* (New York, NY: Random House, Inc., 2019), s.v. "Golgotha," https://www.dictionary.com/browse/golgotha.

Chapter 2

1. Princeton's WordNet, s.v. "condemnation," https://www.definitions.net/definition/condemnation.

2. Thesaurus.net, s.v. "condemnation" synonym, https://www.thesaurus.net/condemnation.

3. *The KJV New Testament Greek Lexicon*, s.v. "katakrino," Strong's #2632, https://www.biblestudytools.com/lexicons/greek/kjv/katakrino.html.

4. *NAS Exhaustive Concordance of the Bible* (LaHabra, CA: The Lockman Foundation, 1981), s.v. "katakrima," Strong's #2631.

5. Thesaurus.com, based on *Roget's 21st Century Thesaurus*, 2nd ed. (Wingdale, NY: The Philip Lief Group, Inc., 2013), s.v. "condemnation" antonym.

6. *The Passion Translation Bible* (Savage, MN: BroadStreet Publishing Group, LLC, 2017), pp. 410–411, *h* in commentary notes.

7. Dictionary.com, s.v. "no," https://www.dictionary.com/browse/no?s=t.

8. *Merriam-Webster Online*, s.v. "no" synonym, https://www.merriam-webster.com/thesaurus/no.

Chapter 3

1. *The Passion Translation Bible*, p. 812, footnote *c*.
2. *NAS Exhaustive Concordance*, s.v. "rabats," Strong's #7257.
3. Ibid., s.v. "nahal," Strong's #5095.
4. Ibid., s.v. "menuchah," Strong's #4496.
5. Max Lucado, *Traveling Light: Releasing the Burdens You Were Never Intended to Bear* (Nashville, TN: Thomas Nelson, Inc., 2006).
6. Dictionary.com, s.v. "peace," https://www.dictionary.com/browse/peace.
7. *NAS Exhaustive Concordance*, s.v. "shuwb," Strong's #7725.
8. Ibid., s.v. "nacham," Strong's #5162.

Chapter 4

1. Paul Ellis, "The Axe of Forgiveness," *Escape to Reality* (blog), December 24, 2010, https://escapetoreality.org/2010/12/24/the-axe-of-forgiveness/.
2. *Thayer's Greek Lexicon*, s.v. "katharizo," Strong's #2511, https://biblehub.com/greek/2511.htm.
3. Thesaurus.com, s.v. "cleanse" synonyms, https://www.thesaurus.com/browse/cleanse?s=t.
4. Dictionary.com, s.v. "flaw," https://www.dictionary.com/browse/flaw?s=t.
5. Thesaurus.com, s.v. "flaw" synonyms, https://www.thesaurus.com/browse/flaw?s=t.
6. Dictionary.com, s.v. "defect," https://www.dictionary.com/browse/defect?s=t.
7. Ibid., s.v. "complete," https://www.dictionary.com/browse/complete?s=t.
8. Thesaurus.com, s.v. "complete" synonyms, https://www.thesaurus.com/browse/complete?s=t.

Chapter 5

1. *NASB Greek Lexicon*, s.v. "exaleipho," Strong's #1813, https://biblehub.com/lexicon/colossians/2-14.htm.
2. "Colossians 2:14–15 Commentary," PreceptAustin.org, updated April 2, 2019, https://www.preceptaustin.org/colossians_214-151#cancelled.
3. Dictionary.com, s.v. "obliterate," https://www.dictionary.com/browse/obliterate.

4. Thesaurus.com, s.v. "obliterate" synonyms, https://www.thesaurus.com/browse/obliterate.

5. "Greek Word Studies: 'Cancel Out,'" Sermonindex.net, http://www.sermonindex.net/modules/articles/index.php?view=article&aid=33670.

6. James Strong, *Strong's Exhaustive Concordance of the Bible* (Nashville, TN: Thomas Nelson, Inc., 1990), Greek Dictionary #5055, s.v. "tetelestai."

7. Hank Lindstrom, "Contrast Law vs. Grace," Bibleline Ministries, http://www.biblelineministries.org/articles/basearch.php?action=full&mainkey=CONTRAST+LAW+VS.+GRACE.

Chapter 6

1. Thesaurus.com, s.v. "permanent" synonyms, https://www.thesaurus.com/browse/permanent.

2. Ibid., s.v. "marvelous" synonyms, https://www.thesaurus.com/browse/marvelous?s=t.

3. Ibid., s.v. "kindness" synonyms, https://www.thesaurus.com/browse/kindness?s=t.

4. *Strong's*, Hebrew Dictionary #1576, s.v. "gemul."

5. Dictionary.com, s.v. "recompense," https://www.dictionary.com/browse/recompense.

Chapter 7

1. Dr. Henry Cloud, "How to Forgive When It's Hard to Forget," Boundaries Books, September 25, 2017, https://www.boundariesbooks.com/boundaries/how-to-forgive-hard-to-forget/.

Chapter 8

1. C. Truman Davis, "A Physician's View of the Crucifixion of Jesus Christ," Christian Broadcasting Network, Inc., http://www1.cbn.com/medical-view-of-the-crucifixion-of-jesus-christ.

2. *Strong's*, Hebrew Dictionary #7665, s.v. "shabar."

3. *NAS Exhaustive Concordance*, s.v. "shabar," Strong's #7665.

4. Kenneth Wuest, *The New Testament: An Expanded Translation* (Grand Rapids/Cambridge: Wm. B. Eerdmans Publishing Co., 1961), John XI, p. 242.

5. *Strong's*, Greek Dictionary #2390, s.v. "iaomai."

6. Ibid., #2616, s.v. "katadunasteuo."

7. *NAS Exhaustive Concordance*, s.v. "katadunasteuo," Strong's #2616.

8   *Strong's*, Greek Dictionary #1411, s.v. "dynamei."

9. Ibid., #3874, s.v. "paraklesis."

10. Ibid., #3870, s.v. "parakaleo."

11. *Merriam-Webster Online*, s.v. "come," https://www.merriam-webster.com/dictionary/come.

Conclusion

1. Charles Spurgeon, "Prodigal Love for the Prodigal Son," sermon #2236, delivered on March 29, 1891, http://www.spurgeongems.org/vols37-39/chs2236.pdf.

2. Matt Williams, "The Prodigal Son's Father Shouldn't Have Run!," *Biola Magazine*, Summer 2010, http://magazine.biola.edu/article/10-summer/the-prodigal-sons-father-shouldnt-have-run/.

Hold On to Hope

Paperback Book

Price: $14.99

Order Now at
nicholemarbach.com
or
amazon.com

Nichole's powerful true story, *Hold On to Hope*, is a page turner that takes you inside her remarkable life journey, demonstrating that no one is beyond hope. You'll walk hand in hand with Nichole through her traumatic childhood into a life of triumph. Her story will bring you encouragement as you realize there's victory available for every trauma, incurable illness, addiction, rejection, and heartache; and, there's freedom for every self-destructive loved one who has wandered off the path. In reading *Hold On to Hope*, you'll discover that God is an incredibly Good and Rescuing Father, who leads us into perfect hope, healing, and wholeness in Jesus Christ.

Love Notes to My Beloved

Devotional Paperback Book

75 Love Notes from Heavenly Father's heart to His precious daughters to help heal wounded hearts

Nichole Marbach Ministries

Spreading the Love and Grace of God around the World

Price: $10.99

Order Now at
nicholemarbach.com
or
amazon.com

Love Notes to My Beloved is a series of love letters from God to you. In reading this book, you will feel as though the words are coming straight from the throne of God. This book is designed to give you an inspiring daily reminder of how much your heavenly Father really loves you. You will begin to develop a deeper understanding of how God feels about you; His true, loving nature; who you are in Him; and all the potential He has placed inside you.

Each daily love note includes daily declarations and scriptures.

77 Texts from Heaven

Teen/Young Adult Devotional Book

Price: $13.99

**Order Now at
nicholemarbach.com
or
amazon.com**

77 Texts from Heaven is a devotional book designed to help teens and young adults come into a deeper revelation of the love and goodness of God. This book has daily nuggets of "good news" for the readers, along with journaling exercises and scriptures to meditate on. Although this devotional can be viewed as targeting teens and youth, all who read it will be inspired and encouraged from its content. It will deeply motivate people to pursue the loving heart of God.

Each daily devotional includes declarations and scriptures.

Made in the USA
Columbia, SC
24 March 2023

14211035R00102